This book belongs to

_____

Write your name now
and take mastery of the contents!

"Simple and easy. It is very good to learn how to write the letters and connect them. I would definitely recommend this..."

Marina Saleeb, USC student

"It was very explicit. It drills things into your head well. It makes Arabic easy to learn. Simplifies what is generally perceived as a difficult language."

Amy Herrmann, USC student

"I like the creativity of the ways to learn the letters and the integration of the Arabic letters into the pictures. It is a unique and creative way to learn the Arabic Alphabet."

Travis, USC student

"Different. Very creative.
...It's a different and creative way to learn Arabic."

Alex, USC student

"Teaches the alphabet in a novel way, instead of just by rote. It's an easy way to learn the Arabic alphabet that isn't boring."

Otis Clarke, USC student

"I liked the visual, oral combination. By combining the visual of writing it and listening to it, I learn it better. Also, the names (Meem Mung bean sprouts) & Genie would definitely help learners remember. Definitely sticks in mind.
...I would say that it is very accessible, it is easy to learn and remember the letters. Good for learning on your own, too."

Catherine Lyons, USC student

Actually
Learn Arabic Letters

A Fun Course That Works--In 3 Weeks

Week 2
Roh' through Ghein
with *four bonus symbols*

by Real World Peace

AUTHORITY BOOKS, INC. AUSTIN, TX

Real World Peace is dedicated to promoting pragmatic, sustainable peace in the real world through enabling communication; raising standards of living; creating basic understanding; and giving people the tools they need to run their own lives well. For more information, please go to http://www.realworldpeace.org

Actually Learn Arabic Letters
A Fun Course That Works--In 3 Weeks
Week 2 Roh' through Ghein *with four bonus symbols*
by Real World Peace

Ⓐ
Published by Authority Books, Inc.
Premiere Edition / First Printing, 2009

Please write the publisher if you are interested in developing this material or if you have further needs.

Authority Books, Inc.
100 Congress Ave Suite 1100
Austin, TX
78701-4042
United States of America
http://www.authoritybooks.com

ISBN-13: 978-1-886275-03-4
(ISBN-10: 1-886275-03-3)

Go ahead and check out
http://www.authoritybooks.com/arabic.html
for some free stuff that will help you out.

Authority
Books

Welcome **Back** to the next part of an exciting
adventure-- one that will last you well for the rest of your life.
You are well on your way. So far you've already finished finding out
about 'Aalif through Dhaal. You've learned how to read and write the
three short vowel marks, plus shad-dah. And you've even found out
how to pronounce **dark** consonant sounds, in a hollow voice in the back
of your mouth. You've learned all this already! Congratulations!

Now, you're ready to start finding out about the next section of the
Arabic alphabet. In this book you're going to learn some of the most
interesting letters in Arabic, including ªein and ghein. You'll learn more
dark letters. And you'll find out how to read, write, and pronounce the
tanween, the grammar marks that come at the end of some words.

This will put you well on your way to gaining command over the Arabic
alphabet. Then, you can show off to your friends what you can do.
Lots of people say this is simply the best book on learning Arabic.
After you finish the easy exercises, and see how fun it is to play with
the letters--and how easy it is to remember them afterwards--maybe
you'll want to say that too. It's because, after you finish filling in
all the fun exercises, you will achieve mastery over the letters in
the Arabic alphabet. You will be able to call each one out by name.
You will be able to read each letter, and say its sound.
And yes, you will even be able to write the letters yourself.

You will

Actually Learn Arabic Letters!

Acknowledgments

This second volume is dedicated to Dr. Jeffrey Magee, whose key insights and wisdom are allowing us to reach the people who need us the most. You have helped so many.

Many thanks are due to Imam Jihad Turk, Director of Religious Affairs at the Islamic Center of Southern California, President of the Wilshire Center Interfaith Council, Vice President of the Interreligious Council of Southern California, and Arabic instructor at UCLA, for his kind words of encouragement, and for opening up his Arabic class to checking out the books. Prof. Turk's constant struggle against violence and hatred, and for peace and understanding, serve as a quiet example for all who work with him.

Many thanks are also due to PhD candidate Sarah Ouwayda of the USC Linguistics Department, for laboriously reviewing the text of all three books; for offering countless suggestions and improvements on how the course instructions could be made better; and for kindly opening up her USC Arabic class to testing out the course.

To Sara Al-Faresi, Vice President of Foreign Affairs of the National Union of Kuwaiti Students USA, thank you for believing in the project and for opening up your conference to the group.

To the Arabic students of USC and UCLA who so graciously served as test subjects, gave comments, and kindly allowed their names to be used, we are truly grateful. In alphabetical order: Alex (USC), Otis Clarke (USC), Eddie (UCLA), Amy Herrmann (USC), Catherine Lyons (USC), Kamal Moummad (UCLA), Wendy Radwan (UCLA), Marina Saleeb (USC), and Travis (USC). To the numerous other students who helped out and chose to remain anonymous we also offer a hearty thank you.

Any mistakes that may remain in the book are of course our fault, and not the responsibility of any of these busy commentators who kindly offered their time to advise on sections of early versions.

Mr. Johnny Casey and his base team deserve extra praise for work above and beyond the call of duty, and for providing support during the dark hours.

Exquisite thanks are due to cartoonist Phillip Shrock for his pencils and inks of the funny pictures, and for making the vision real.

Beautiful thanks are due to graphic designer Audrey Snodgrass, for her work on the third version of the covers. Graphic designer Lisa Yu worked tirelessly on much of the intricate writing instructions art work, and provided the gorgeous second edition of the covers. Rachel Hamm, Amber Howell, and Gayle Cantrell were all instrumental in pushing through the production. Great thanks go to Gay Alano for payroll, taxes, and outstanding strategic financial planning. Finally, to all the rest of the Real World Peace and Authority Books teams, many of whom believed in the project enough to sign up for deferred payment--the graphic design team, the writing team, editing, layout and production, the testing team, the marketing group, and the computer support team--hearty thanks is presented. We couldn't have done it without you.

Review Of
A Quick Summary for Smart People

Let's jump right in! Here's a review of the handful of basic facts you need to know eventually about how Arabic works. Maybe you've learned these already, or maybe not. They're still good to review. And don't worry if you don't understand these fully right now. Just run your eyes over them and read these facts for now, and what they actually mean will become clear to you later on.

1. Arabic reads right-to-left on a line. Then the lines go top-to-bottom. After you get used to this, it's no problem.

2. Arabic is written in *script letters* (not BLOCK LETTERS). So they're connected.

3. There are NO Capital Letters.

4. Instead of Capital and small letters, there are four slightly different forms for each letter. These depend on whether the letter is *standing alone* by itself, is *starting* the word, is in the *middle* of the word, or is at the *end* of the word. We will cleverly call these the Stand-Alone Form, the Beginning Form, the Middle Form and the Ending Form, so that you can tell them apart easily. In most cases, many of these will be almost exactly the same inside one letter, so it's no big deal. Certainly it's no worse than, say, having to learn Capital "A" and small "a", I mean, they kind of look like each other but kind of look different. It's the same in Arabic. Usually the Stand-Alone form will be the fanciest, it is kind of like what we think of when we write Capital initials in script. It's the "official" portrait of the letter. Usually the Ending Form will look a lot like the Stand-Alone Form, except of course it has to be connected from the previous letter.
The Beginning Form usually looks like a shorter, more simple version, and the Middle Form often looks like the Beginning Form. You'll see.
Remember that the beginning is on the right, and the end of the word is on the left.

A Quick Summary for Smart People (continued)

5. Almost all of the official Arabic letters are **consonants**.

6. There are only three "long" vowels in the official alphabet:
    "aa" (A),   "ii" (or "ee") (y),   and   "uu" (or "oo") (w).

7. There are only three "short" vowels:
    "a" ,   "i" (or "e"),   and   "u" (or "o").

8. Short vowels are written using "accents" (diacritic marks).
    Short vowels are not part of the official alphabet.
    Short vowels are typically **not written** in normal text for adults,
    because everyone knows what they are, anyway.

9. The long vowels are pronounced longer in time than the short vowels.
    That's why they're called "long". And that's why they're written in
    English with double letters. The sound is supposed to be the same, though.

10. Certain irregular forms, such as taa marbuuta, can also count as vowels
    such as "ah". This will all be covered later.

11. There is always a good-sized space **between** words. Just like in English.

12. **Inside** a single word, most letter forms are **connected** to the next letter
    following on the left. However, a few aren't. Like an English script *O*
    (Capital O), the letter finishes, there's a small space, and then the next
    letter has to start up again by itself. It's an **unconnected** letter.
    This will be important.

13. The next letter that follows a "connected letter" is in the Middle Form,
    because it's in the middle of the word. Unless it's on the end, of course.

14. The next letter that follows an "unconnected letter" has to start over and
    be in the *Starting Form*, because it doesn't have any line coming into it.
    Even if it's in the middle of the word. If on the end, use *Stand-Alone Form*.

Actually
Learn Arabic Letters

A Fun Course That Works--In 3 Weeks

Week 2
Roh' through Ghein
with *four bonus symbols*

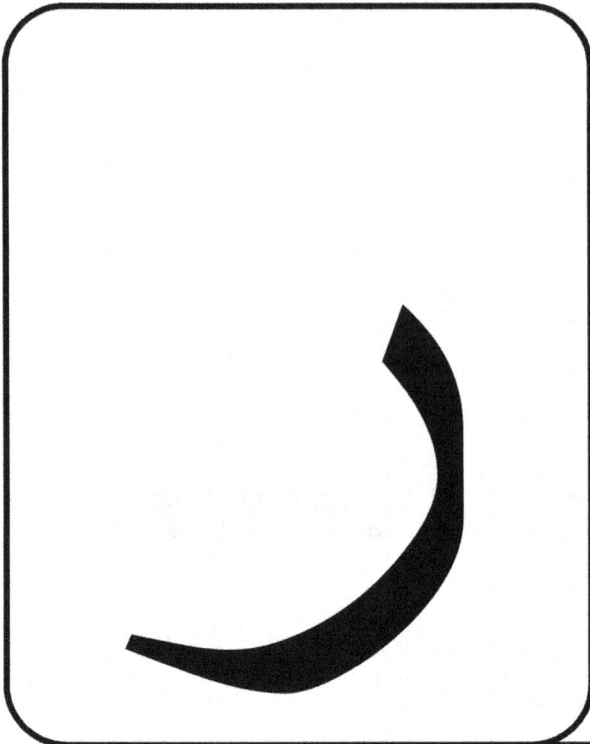

Roh'

R

ر

ر | ـر | ـرـ

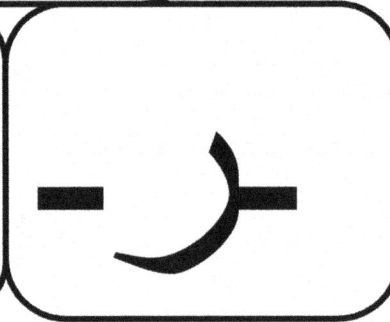

"alveolar trill"

راء

Roh', sometimes spelled raa', is pronounced as a rolled "r".
It is basically similar to the Spanish "rr".
...Roh' is a "dark letter", pronounced with a hollow throat, that
turns a following "ah" vowel into something closer to an "Oh".

r   *Roh' CONNECTS on the left.*   r, R

Roh'

is the rowing oar

Row, row, row your boat
Racing through the brine
A single oar all by itself
Is rah! rah! All the time.

Helpful Hints

Of course a Rowing Oar has to be underwater for it to work properly, with a handle sticking out above the water. And so the Roh' is about two-thirds under the line, if you look at it vertically. That's the oar. And it has about one-third going above the line. That's the handle.

Rrememberr that Rroh' is *always* prronounced with a rrolled rr sound. The tip of yourr tongue bounces rrapidly against the rroof of yourr mouth.

There is no single-click "r" in Arabic as there is in Spanish (or Japanese). Just the rolled "R", only one. So you don't need to worry about the difference between different r's.

Arabic "gh", which we'll cover later on in this book, is pronounced by rolling the *back of your throat*, not the tip of your tongue. It's different.

Roh' is a dark consonant that is pronounced in a hollow voice by keeping the back of your throat open. This then turns any following 'Aalif "ah" sound into a hollow "aw"/"oh" sound. Think of how the vohmpirres from Trrrohnsylvohnioh sound, in their hollow voices. Bwoh'-hoh'-hoh'.

So the name for "Roh'" or "Raa'" is actually spelled with a Roh'-'Aalif. But it's pronounced closer to a deep Rah' or Roh'.

The name for "Rah" sounds a lot like the Greek name rho (ρ). If you spell it backwards, it turns into "ahR", which is how we say it. Since lots of things in Arabic are backwards from English, this makes sense.

We'll try to spell Roh' with a capital letter, to remind you it's dark.

Roh' is the most common letter in the Arabic dictionary. It shows up in 24% of all words.

Now You Sketch It--Doodles!

How To Write It

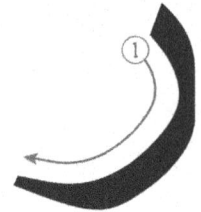

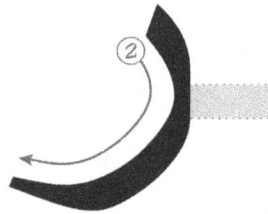

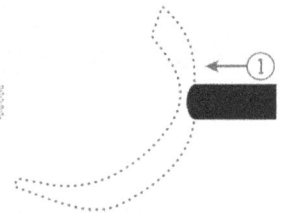

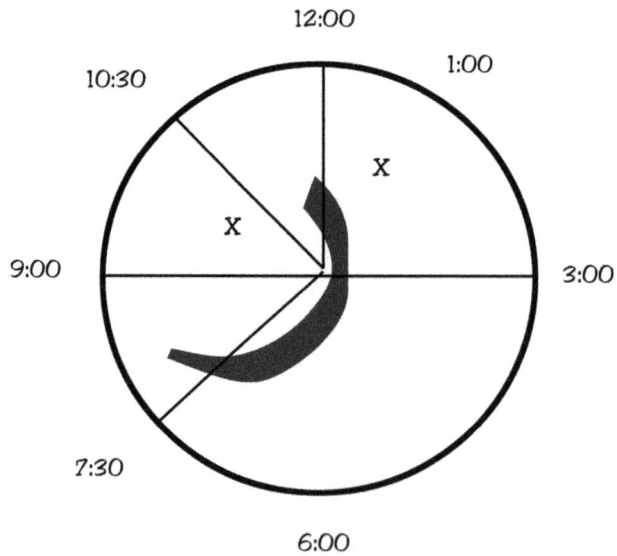

Writing Suggestions

Stand-Alone Form

1. Roh' is a single swish that starts up about one-third of the way up above the line, and comes down descending to about two-thirds of the way below the line. It is concave bending outwards, like a rubber oar. The "handle" of the oar can start somewhere at an angle between 10:30 and 12:00 on the clock, but you never want it to start back past 12:00 going to 1:00, nor deeper than 10:30 going to 9:00. The "oar" should curve down at 7:30. If you have a caligraphy brush, when you pull up off the paper it will make a little tiny line, a serif, that simply emphasizes the end. On the fancy type-fonts this will add a little extra line that hooks slightly upwards, as you can see, but it's not necessary to put this in on your handwritten versions.

Beginning Form

Same as the Stand-Alone Form, with a short space. Roh' is not connected on the left, so restart the next letter with a Beginning Form, even when it's in the middle of the word. **The following space is part of the letter**--but not the extra bar used here to show it.

Middle Form

1. You're coming in from the previous letter. Draw a flat bar that's on the line.
2. Starting one-third of the way up, and slightly forward, draw a swooping stroke that connects with the previous bar, and continues on downwards to two-thirds of the way below the line.
3. Leave a short space, less than the space between two words, and continue on with the Beginning Form of the next letter, even though it's in the middle of the word.

Ending Form

Same as the Middle Form. Leave a long space **between** words. It's longer than the short space that you use after the Beginning/Middle Forms **inside** words until the next letter.

7

Writing Practice

Say the name of the letter, and make its sound,
each time you write the letter.

Writing Practice

Now put them together.
Remember to keep each letter
separate in your mind.

We're going to cheat here with unconnected Roh' by putting an extra hyphen bar between the Beginning and Middle, and the Middle and Ending forms, for practice only. This is better for beginners, but it doesn't actually make much sense. Your teacher might insist on you putting a baa' or a yaa' or something in between instead.

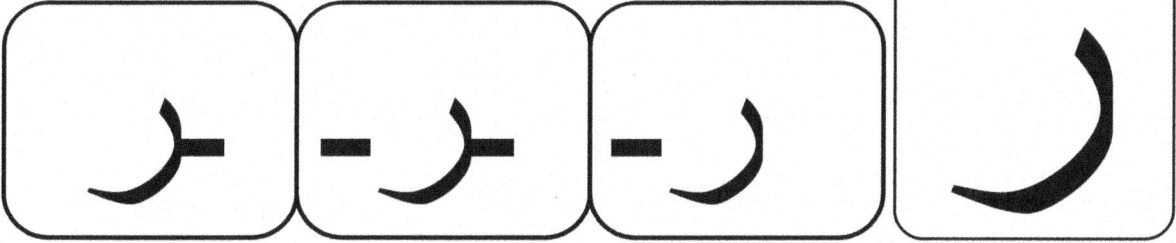

ر-	ر- ر-	ر- ر-	ر

Know The Difference!

Zaay has the zy-zy bug jumping on top of the zooming fish.	ز
Daal is bending into a duck shape.	د
Meem has a mung-bean root that goes straight down.	م
The pool ending-shape on Saad, Seen, and Noon is deep and round, not a short Rowing oaR.	س ص ن
ªein curves backwards to the right, not forwards to the left.	ع ع
Wow has a loop at the top for the Wide White toWel. It is used as a vowel.	و

Reading Practice

رَدَّ

a 2 d a R
Radda
to send/take/give back

رَجا

A j a R
Rajaa
to hope for

سَرير

R y R a s
saReeR
bed

رادار

R A d A R
RaadaaR
radar

zaay

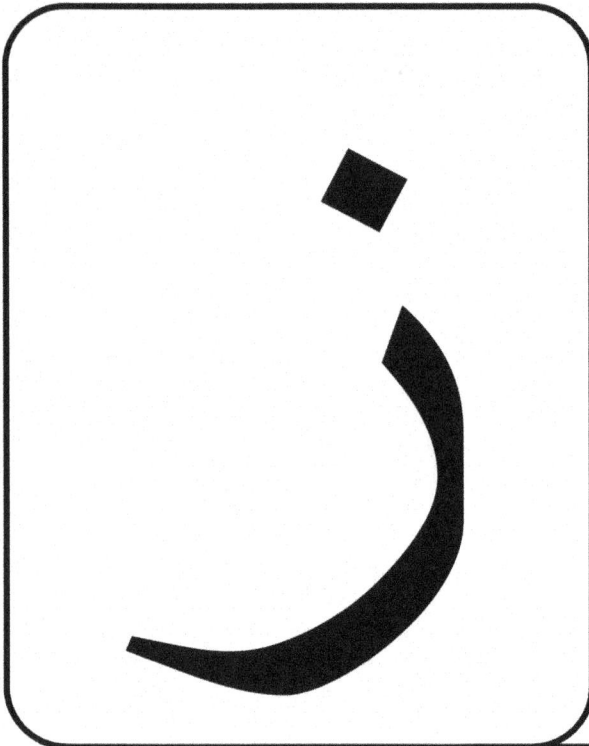

Z

"voiced alveolar fricative"

زاي

Zaay is pronounced like the familiar "z".
It's a light sound that comes from the front of the mouth.

zaay
is the whizzing Zy-Zy bug

Zoom!
It's the whizzing
Zy-Zy bug
Zorching out of the sky!
With amazing streak
He protects the weak
As fishes wish **they** could fly.

Helpful Hints

Zaay is just like the letter Roh', except it has an extra dot on top.

The fish is two-thirds of the way underwater. His head is jumping up one-third of the way out of the water, trying to catch the bug.

Remember that pronouncing a "z" is similar to pronouncing a buzzed "s". Just like the difference between "th" and "dh", it uses your voice. Zaay is a light, normal "z", and it comes from the front of your mouth, with your tongue behind your teeth.

"Zaay" rhymes with "my". It looks a little bit similar to Greek zeta (ζ), which also has a tick-mark (turned into a bar) on top of a jumping fish shape, but the fish is backwards. This is a small zeta. In order to make this a capital Zeta (Z), the fish became more angular, with a corner at the bottom. This gave us our letter "Z". Zoom!

Now You Sketch It--Doodles!

How To Write It

Writing Suggestions

ﺯ - ﺯ - ﺯ

Stand-Alone Form
1. Starting one-third of the way up above the line, draw a swooping stroke down to two-thirds of the way below the line. This is the jumping fish.
2. Put a dot on top of the fish's head. This is the zooming zy-zy bug that the fish is chasing.

Beginning Form
Same as the stand-alone form. Leave a short space, shorter than the space between words. The space is part of the letter zaay. Start the next letter with its Beginning Form as well, even though it's in the middle of the word. We use an underscore bar here to show you where the next letter goes.

Middle Form
1. You're coming in from the previous letter on the right. Draw a straight bar on the line.
2. Go up one-third above the line, and draw a sweeping curve downwards. Make sure you connect up with the bar, but don't leave a gap, and don't cross it like a "t"--just brush past it, like the side of an "H".
3. Leave a small space, and continue on with the Beginning Form of the next letter. Whatever that next letter is, is represented here by the underscore bar.
4. Come back *later* and dot the zaay with a small dot above the fish's head.

Ending Form
Same as the Middle Form. Leave a longer space after the letter between words.

Writing Practice

Say the name of the letter, and make its sound,
each time you write the letter.

Writing Practice

Now put them together.
Remember to keep each letter
separate in your mind.

Zaay is another of the few unconnected letters that we're going to have to cheat on in order to practice connecting the Middle and Ending forms up. So we introduce an additional extra hyphen bar for practice only. Normally the middle form would have to start over with the Beginning, and the last form would have to be a Stand-Alone...

ـزـ	ـزـ	ـز	ز

Know The Difference!

Roh' the Rowing oaR has no zooming zy-zy bug on top.	ر
Wow the Wide White toWel has a loop at the top, and no dot.	و
dhaal the souTHern moTHer duck is duck-shaped, flat, with a small bent-upwards duck-tail.	ذ
Beginning noon does not extend below the line, and it's connected on the left to the following letter.	نـ
Khaa' looks like Khan's Khap. It also does not extend below the line, and is connected to the next letter on the left.	خـ
Ghein bends backwards to the right, not forwards to the left, and has a loop at the top.	غـ

Reading Practice

جَوز

z w a j
jawz
a pair of

زَيت

t y a z
zayt
oil

زَوج

j w a z
zawj
partner, spouse;
husband

أُرزّ

2 z R a
aRuzz
rice

seen

س

s

"voiceless alveolar fricative"

سين

seen is pronounced just like the familiar "s" sound.
It comes from the front of your mouth,
with the tip of your tongue behind your teeth.
It's a "light" sound.

S   *seen CONNECTS on the left.*   S

seen

is the silly glasses

seen.
seen.
seen.
Say, has
Sue seen?

Six hissing snails
slip
through
the green!

sssss

ssssss

sssss

Helpful Hints

seen is the silly eyeglasses. The ending and stand-alone forms have a big handle.

seen is different from other letters because there are three bumps all in a row. These form a pattern that is easy to recognize. After you know what to look for, it will jump out at you. Then you will say, "I see the **seen**!".

seen looks almost like a sideways version of the Greek letter Sigma (Σ), which also has three bumps.

The handle is only drawn when you want to get fancy-- at the end, or in the stand-alone version. There's no time to draw the handle at the beginning or in the middle of a word.

In handwriting, usually the three bumps are flattened out. The entire letter up to the handle is simply replaced with a long straight line on the line.

The letter "s" for "seen" is always written as a small "s" when you write it down in English letters. This is to keep you from confusing it with a different letter, Sod, called the "dark S". Sod is written as a capital "S". We'll be studying Sod pretty soon in this book.

Now You Sketch It--Doodles!

How To Write It

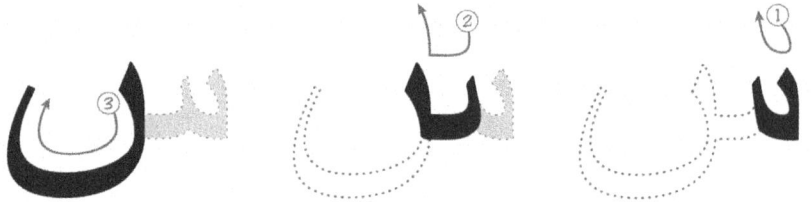

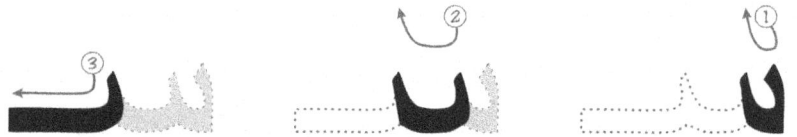

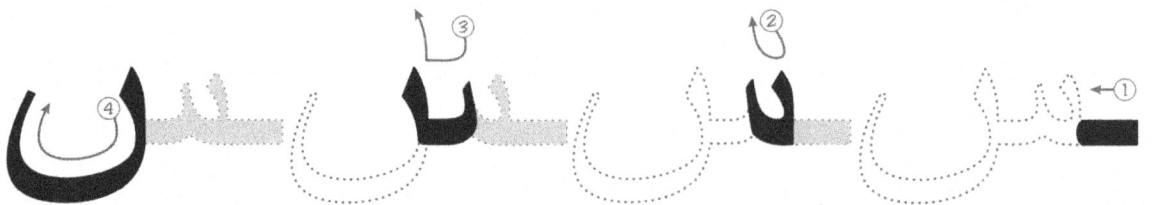

Writing Suggestions

Stand-Alone Form
1. Start drawing the seen silly glasses on the right side. Start about one-quarter of the way up, above the line. Draw a swooping loop down onto the line, then back up again to the left. This forms the first side of the glasses.
2. Draw a second loop down to the line, and back up again. Make the end come up about as high as the other two bumps to make it look good. This forms the second side of the glasses.
3. Now draw a big handle shape. This is an important part of the Stand-Alone Form for the letter "seen". Make it a big bowl shape that curves down, is kind of flat on the bottom, and curves back up again--almost like a sideways "C". The left end should go back up again at least as far as the line, if not a little bit higher. This is a big loop--as big as the other two loops put together.

Beginning Form
1. Start about one-fourth of the way above the line. Draw a loop down to the line, and then back up again. That's the first side of the silly glasses.
2. Draw another loop down to the line and back up again. That's the second side of the silly glasses. Sometimes the top of the second half of this loop will actually lean in to the right slightly, to show that all three peaks are together in one letter.
3. Finish the third peak by going back down to the line. Continue on the line on to the next letter, represented here by a generic straight bar.

Middle Form
1. You're coming in from the right, on the line.
2. Go up and form the first peak, and then the first loop, into the second peak.
3. Form the second loop from the second peak into the third peak. Keep the bottom of the loop flat on the line. The second loop is just slightly wider than the first loop. The third peak can lean to the right.
4. Come down from the third peak, and continue on the line on to the next letter, here shown by a bar.

Ending Form
1, 2 You're coming in from the right, on the line. Go up and form the first peak. Loop for the next peak.
3,4. Go up and form the third peak. Finish like the Stand-Alone Form. The third peak leans slightly to the left. Make sure to make a nice bowl shape for the handle--it finishes at the line or slightly above.

Writing Practice

Say the name of the letter, and make its sound,
each time you write the letter.

Writing Practice

Now put them together.
Remember to keep each letter
separate in your mind.

*Since seen is actually connected, we don't need to cheat any more
here, nor with the rest of the alphabet letters in this book. The
connections between the script letters are supposed to be there.*

سـس	ـسـ	ـس	س

Know The Difference!

Sheen is three diamonds shine more on the shimmers by the shore. Sheen has three dots.	ش
taa', Thaa', or Noon are single spikes that have dots at the top.	ت ـنـ ث
Final Noon has a handle but no silly spectacles. It also has a geNie Navel dot.	ن
Baa' and Yaa' are single spikes that have dots at the bottom. These spikes do not come together in a set of three like the Silly Spectacles.	بـ ي
Qaaf has a loop up top, along with a queen's crown of two dots.	ق
ᵃein curves backwards to the right and has only one hook up top, used as a shephard's crook for bleating lambs.	ع

Reading Practice

إسم

m s i
ism
given name

سِنّ

2 n i s
sinn
~ years old

قسيس

s y s Q
Qis-sees
priest

سكر

R k s
suk-kaR
sugar

(The last snail is carrying his S cargo.)

sheen

sh

ش

ث ث ش

ـش ـشـ ـشـ ش

ش

"voiceless palato-alveolar fricative"

شين

Sheen sounds like the familiar "sh".

sh   Sheen CONNECTS on the left.   sh/š

34

sheen
is the shiny shades

Sheen.
Sheen.
Sheen.
Three diamonds
shine more.

She
shapes
shimmers
by the
shore.

35

Helpful Hints

Sheen is just exactly like seen, except it has the extra three shiny diamonds up top. These are the same three diamonds that we saw on thaa'. No other letters in Arabic except thaa' and sheen have these three diamonds, so these are easy to recognize.

In handwriting, not only do the three bumps become a single long line, as in *seen*, but people decided it took too long to make the three dots. So the three dots get re-placed by a caret (^) that looks like the top two sides of a triangle.

Now You Sketch It--Doodles!

How To Write It

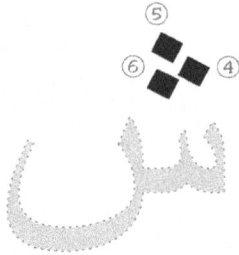

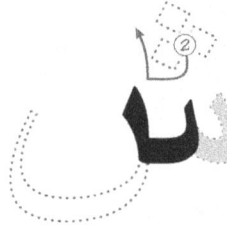

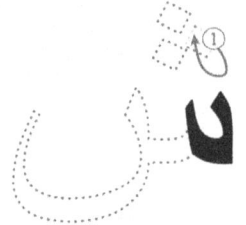

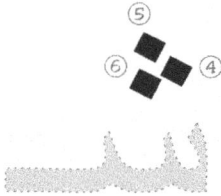

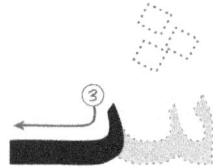

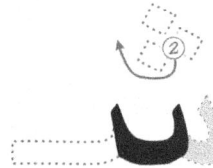

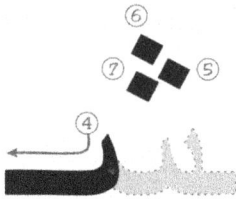

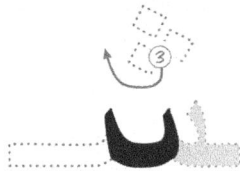

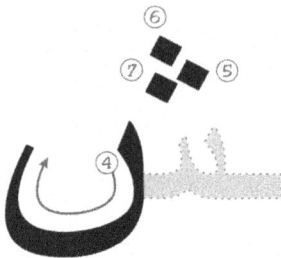

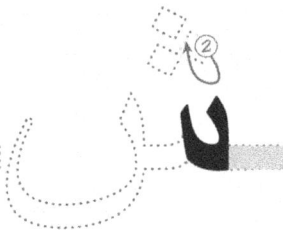

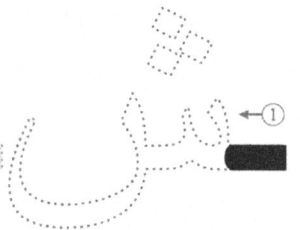

38

Writing Suggestions

ش شـ شـ

Stand-Alone Form

1. From a quarter of the way up, draw the first peak, down to the line, up to the second peak.
2. Draw the second loop of the shiny shades slightly wider. The third peak tilts to the left.
3. Draw the big cup, which is the handle for the shiny shades. The bottom of the handle is slightly flat, and the end comes back up just above the line.
4, 5, 6. Draw the right dot, the middle upper dot, and the left dot in a tight triangular pattern just above the middle of the sheen. The order is important. They should be centered around the middle peak.

Beginning Form

1. From a quarter of the way up, draw the 1st peak, loop down to the line, up to the next peak.
2. Draw the second loop of the shiny shades. Loop down to the line, and up to the third peak. The second loop is slightly wider than the first. The third peak can tilt slightly left or right.
3. Continue on to the next letter, here represented by a generic bar.
4, 5, 6. Later on, come back and put in the three dots. They are centered above the 2nd peak.

Middle Form

1. You are coming in from the right from the previous letter, on the line.
2. Go up a quarter of the way, and draw the first loop of the shiny shades down to the line. Continue on with the rest being the same as the Beginning Form.

Ending Form

1. You're coming in from the right from the previous letter, on the line.
2. Continue on as with the Stand-Alone Form. The third peak tilts slightly to the left, so that the cup of the handle is round. The bottom of the handle is slightly flat, and the end comes back up so that it is just above the line. The three dots in a triangle are over the 2nd peak.

39

Writing Practice

Say the name of the letter, and make its sound,
each time you write the letter.

Writing Practice

Now put them together.
Remember to keep each letter
separate in your mind.

ش	ﺷ	ﺷ	ش
ـش	ـشـ	ـشـ	

Know The Difference!

seen has no three dots at the top. It is simply the Silly Spectacles.	سـ
Thaa' has three dots over a spike, but it's a single spike of Thoth's Thick Thumb. It's not the set of Shimmer Shore Shades with their handle.	ثـ
Stand-alone Thaa' has an open Thawing dish, for its Thought Thistles.	ث
Final Noon has a handle but no Shore Shades. Also it has the geNie Navel single dot.	ن
Yaa' has two dots underneath, and does not have the three wavy peaks of the Shimmer Shore Shades.	يـ
Dod has the handle, but it's beside a Dog on a Dune. No Shades.	ض

Reading Practice

شاءَ

a ' A sh
shaa'a
to want

رَشّ

2 sh a R
Rashsh
splash, spray

شابّ

2 b A sh
shaabb
young; a teenager

ريش

sh y R
Reesh
feathers

غشّاش

sh A 2 sh gh
ghash-shaash
a cheater

شَمس

s m a sh
shams
sun

Sod

S

ص

ص   ـصـ   ـص

"emphatic voiceless alveolar fricative"

صاد

Sod (Saad) is an emphatic, strong, or "dark" S sound. Instead of putting the tip of your tongue behind your teeth, slide it backwards until it's pressing the roof of your mouth. Open the back of your tongue in your throat. Now strongly push out an "S" sound that comes from the back of your throat.

S / 9   *Sod CONNECTS on the left.*   S / ṣ

Sod

is the Sad Sod Sand Dune

Sad. Sad. Sod.

Some Strong Sod Sand Dune
By the Silent Sea Shore
Stands Sadly *Alone*
And there's nothing more.
Strongly Said Sod!

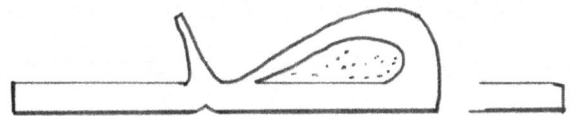

Sod Sand by the Sea--nothing more. How Sad!

Helpful Hints

The dark "S" Sod is pronounced in the back of the mouth. It might help if you think of doing a Humphrey Bogart or a Sean Connery imitation. There is a bubble, a space over the back of your tongue--it's almost like you had an imaginary ping-pong ball stuck in the back of your mouth, keeping things open.

Because the dark letters are pronounced in the back of the throat, any "aa" (like "father") that follows a dark letter turns into an "o" sound (like "hot") when you say it. These are considered to be the same sound in Arabic.

However, we think the dark S "Sod" and the light s "seen" are maybe the same, whereas in Arabic they think they are quite different. So it evens out.

The bowl that comes at the end of Sod is the same shape that you saw for the handle on "seen" and "sheen". You'll be seeing a lot of this bowl shape.

Now You Sketch It--Doodles!

How To Write It

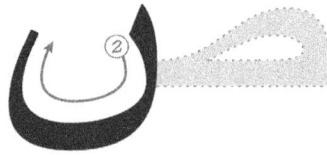

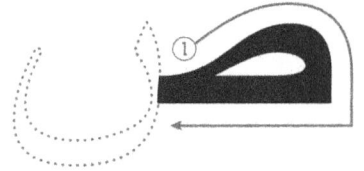

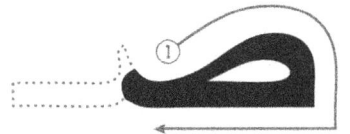

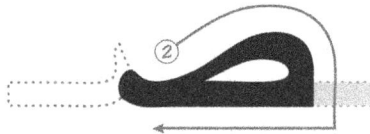

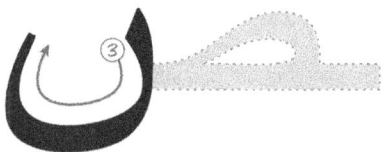

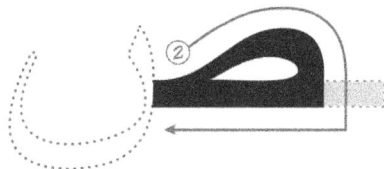

Writing Suggestions

Stand-Alone Form
1. Start on the line, ahead of where you're going to draw. Draw a big swirling upper loop from left to right for the Sad Sod Sand dune. Come down to the line, and pull it in straight on the line to close the loop. The sand dune should be about twice as long as it is tall.
2. Go up a short way above the line, and form the rim of the tidal-pool cup. Continue on down, around, and back up again. This is the Sea by the Sod Sand dune. The rim of the tidal pool is shorter than the top of the Sand dune hill. The Sea tidal pool is cup-shaped, like a sideways "C", a little flat on the bottom. The end of the stroke comes back slightly above the line.

Beginning Form
1. Start on the line, ahead of where you're going to draw. Draw a big swirling upper loop from left to right. Round it on the top, and come down to the line. Pull it in straight along the line to close the loop off. This is the Sod Sand dune.
2. The wave by the Sea is only shown in miniature, as a tiny bump, in the Beginning Form. Continue on, go up just a little bit, and then go back down again. Now continue on to the next letter on the left, represented by the bar on the line. The little wave by the Sea is not as tall as the Sod Sad Sand dune, it's just a tiny bump.

Middle Form
1. You're coming in on the line from the previous letter on the right.
2. Pick up your pen and jump ahead on the line. Now make the swooping, arching loop for the Sod Sand dune, going backwards to the right. Meet up with the end of the previous line. Come forward flat on the line to the left, to form the bottom of the Sod Sad Sand dune.
3. Make the little wave by the Sea, and continue on to the next letter.

Ending Form
1. You're coming in from the right, on the line.
2. Pick up your pen and jump ahead on the line. Draw the Sad Sod Sand Dune.
3. Now draw the tidal pool by the Sea, just like in the Stand-Alone Form.

Writing Practice
Say the name of the letter, and make its sound,
each time you write the letter.

Writing Practice

Now put them together.
Remember to keep each letter
separate in your mind.

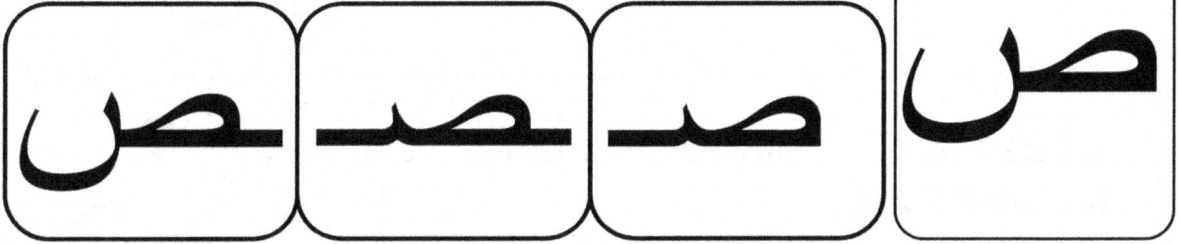

ص	ـصـ	ـصـ	ـص

Know The Difference!

Dod has the Dancing Dog on the Dune. Sod is Sadly all alone, no Dog.	ض
Taa has the Tall Tall Tower right next to the sand dune.	ط
Haa' is open, it has no loop.	ح
Faa' or Qaaf in the middle of a word have a loop, but it's not Sand Dune shape. Also no following little hill-crest.	ـفـ ـقـ
Meem is smaller and rounded-- it is not Sand Dune shape.	ـم
Final or stand-alone Qaaf has a loop at the top and a pool following, but the loop points to the left. Qaaf is also crowned with two points.	ق

Reading Practice

خاصّ

2 S A kh
khaaSS
special, particular

صارَ

a R A S
SaaRa
to become
("que sera, sera")

صُرصور

R w S R u S
SuRSooR
cockroach

صَبَّ

a 2 b a S
Sabba
to pour

رَصاص

S A S a R
RaSaaS
lead (the metal; a pencil's)

Dod

D

ض

ض‍   ‍ض‍   ‍ض

"emphatic voiced alveolar stop" ضاد

Dod (Daad) is pronounced as an emphatic, strong "dark" D. Put the tip of your tongue pressing the roof of your mouth again, and open the back of your throat. Now push out a strong "D".

D/9'   *Dod CONNECTS on the left.*   D/ḍ/ḍ

Dod

is Dad's Dog on the Dune

Dad's Dog on the Dune
And he wants to play
Dancing, Dancing with Delight
Every Dog has his Day!

Dog-star on the Dune

Helpful Hints

Dod looks just like Sod, except with an extra dot on top.

Dod, like Sod, is also a "dark" letter. It's pronounced in the back of the throat. So it also turns a following "aa" sound (as in "father") into an "o" sound (as in "hot"). This is what all of the dark letters do.

Dod is written in English with a capital letter "D". This is to distinguish it from daal, which represents the normal, light letter "d".

Now You Sketch It--Doodles!

How To Write It

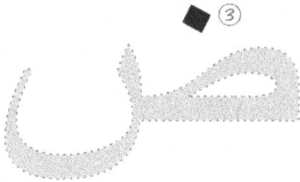

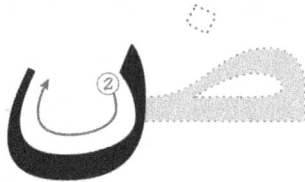

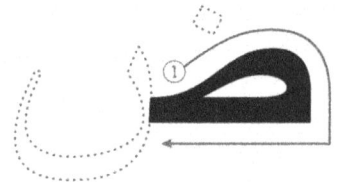

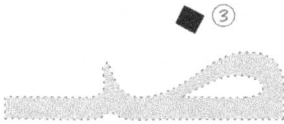

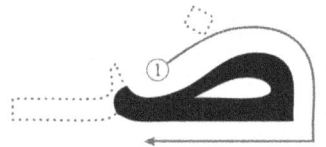

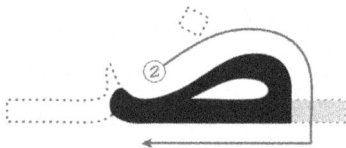

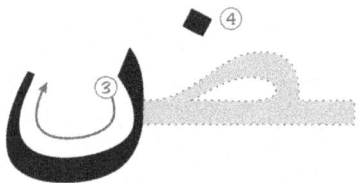

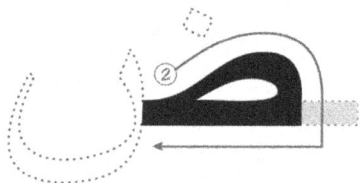

Writing Suggestions

ض ضـ ـضـ ـض

Stand-Alone Form

1. Start on the line, ahead of where you're going to draw. Draw a swirling loop up and back, to the right. Come down to the line. Close the loop by coming in straight on the line from right to left. The loop is twice as wide as it is high.
2. Draw the tidal pool beside the Dune by going up slightly, and then coming around in a big cup shape, like a "C" on its side. The bottom is slightly flat. The end of the stroke comes back up slightly above the line. Make the cup round, like a fish-bowl.
3. Put a dot hovering over the slope of the sand Dune. That's Dad's Dancing Dog. He's on the side of the hill--not up at the top, and not about to be hit by the waves at the edge, either--just jumping up into the air in the middle.

Beginning Form

1. Start on the line, ahead of where you're going to draw. Draw the Dune up, down, and around underneath. Keep flat on the line on the bottom.
2. Draw a little wave to represent the tidal pool at the edge of the Dune. It's not as high as the Dune.
3. Continue on to the left, on to the next letter, shown here by a generic bar.
4. Come back later and put a dot over the side of the hill. That's the Dog on the Dune.

Middle Form

1. You're coming in from the right, in on the line from the previous letter.
2. Pick up your pen. Jump it ahead on the line. Draw a swirling loop back, that goes up, down, and meets up with the previous line. Continue on the line from right to left in order to close the loop, and draw the entire Dune.
3, 4. Continue on with the small wave and the Dog, as with the Beginning Form.

Ending Form

1. You're coming in from the right.
2. Pick up your pen. Jump ahead on the line. Draw the Dune.
3. Continue on by drawing the cup for the tidal pool, as in the Stand-Alone Form.
4. Finish by putting a dot above the side of the Dune hill. That's the Dog on the Dune.

Writing Practice

Say the name of the letter, and make its sound,
each time you write the letter.

Writing Practice

Now put them together.
Remember to keep each letter
separate in your mind.

ض	ـضـ	ـضـ	ضـ

Know The Difference!

Sod is the Sad Sod Sand dune
Standing Sadly Alone by itself.
It is Sadly missing the Dancing Dog.

ص

Zaa' has both the dune and the dog star,
but it is immediately followed by the
strong-Z-snoring watchtower.

ظ

Sheen has the handle or pool to the left,
but it has no Dune. It also has
three dots, not one.

ش

Taa' is the Tall, Tall Tower by the hill.
It has no dot above.

ط

Final Noon has a dot, but it's for the
geNie's Navel, not above the Dune.
There is no Dune at Noon.

ن

Ghein is triangular and does not look
Dune-shaped.

غ

Reading Practice

أرض

D r a
arD
ground

ضِدّ

2 d i D
Didd
opposite, contrary;
against; vs.

ضَباب

b A b a D
Dabaab
mist, fog

ضأن

n ' A D
Daa'n
sheep

ضَحك

k H a D
DaHk
laugh

بَيض

D y a b
bayD
eggs

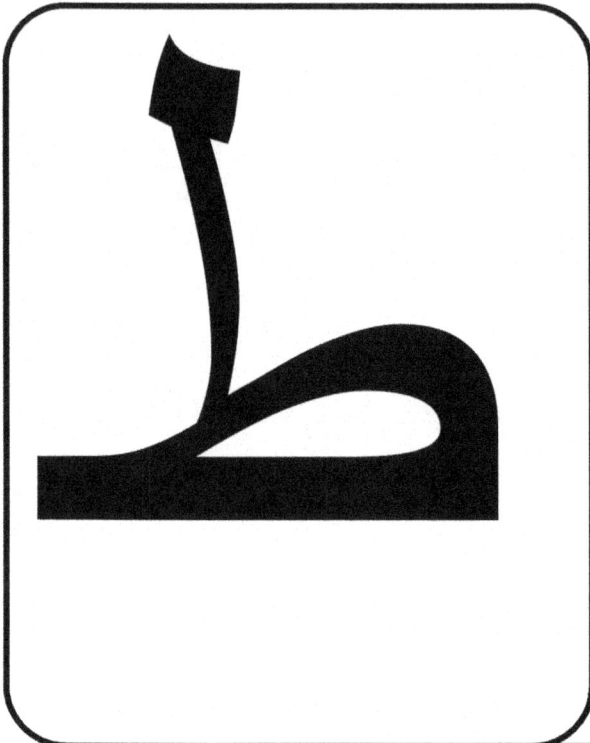

Taa'

ط

T

ط   ط   ط

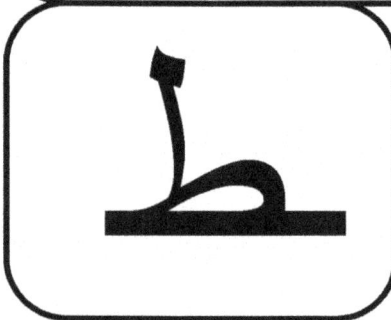

"emphatic voiceless alveolar stop"

طاء

Taa' (or Toh') is pronounced a lot like Dod, except it's a strong, dark "T" sound instead of a "D" sound. Put your tongue in the same place, back up against the roof of your mouth. Open the back of your throat. Now strongly push out a "T" sound. This is called an "emphatic T" or "dark T", because it comes from the back of your throat.

T / 6   *Taa' CONNECTS on the left.*   T/ṭ/ṯ

Taa'
is the Tall, Tall Tower

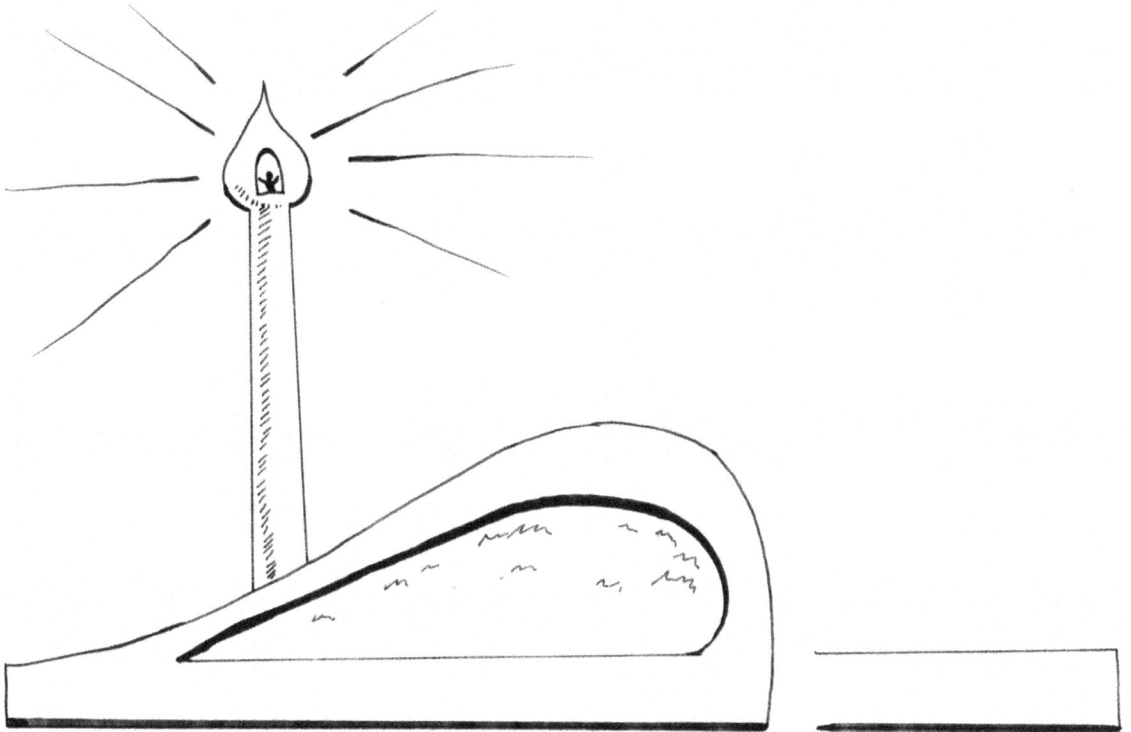

Taa' Taa' Taa'

is a Tall Tall Tower
sTanding *alone* on a hill;
On iTs Top, a Torch is seT
IT's a Tiny minareT,
Calling the faithful to prayer.

Helpful Hints

If you have problems finding the right tongue position, say "Turtle". Try to think of the dark "ur" sound coloring the "T" at the beginning. Say "Tur, Tur, Turtle".
Notice how your tongue is in the back of your mouth.

Now say "tin". Notice how your tongue moves to the front of your mouth when you say the "t". Play back and forth with the difference in the tongue position between "tin" and "Turtle". This will help you with understanding how to pronounce the dark, emphatic "T".

Like all dark letters, an "aa" following a Taa' actually is pronounced like an "o" sound as in "hot".

Now You Sketch It--Doodles!

How To Write It

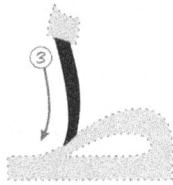

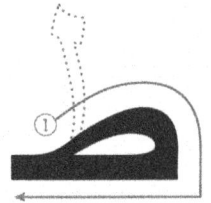

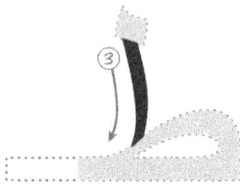

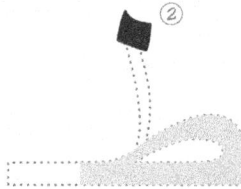

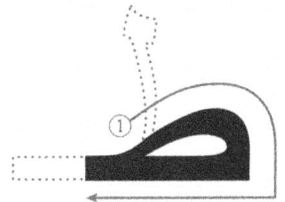

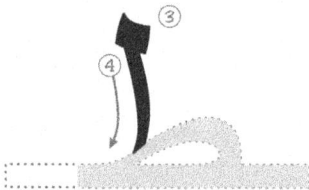

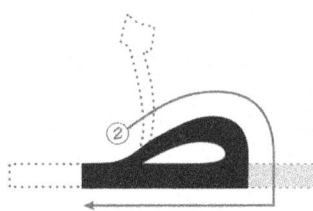

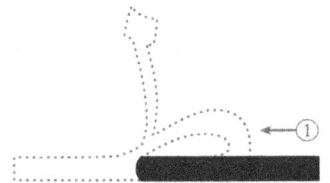

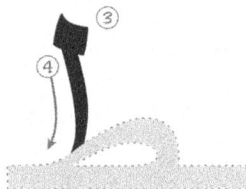

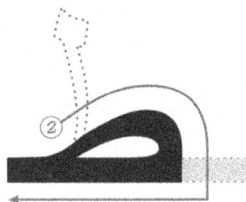

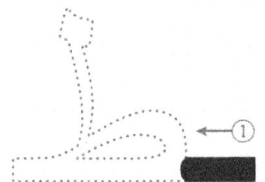

68

Writing Suggestions

ط ط ط

Stand-Alone Form

1. Pick up your pen and jump ahead. Starting on the line, draw a swooping curve up, over, and down. Some people make a hard corner at the line, while others curve and simply continue the loop. Close the loop from right to left on the line, meeting up and crossing where you started. In the Stand-Alone Form, continue on with a short overshoot on the line, so there is a small nub on the left--the bottom line does not stop where the slope of the hill started, but continues on slightly.
2. Pick up your pen and jump it all the way up to the top. Draw a blot, a short serif, or a hook, to start the Tower. This is the Torch on top of the minaret. In printed type, this is an important part of the letter that visually distinguishes it from 'aalif. It's always on signs, in books, etc. So you should learn it, and practice it as you draw. However, in actual handwriting, most people will skip this feature.
3. Draw a straight line downwards onto the side of the hill, just before it meets the bottom plain on the line. The Tower is at the bottom of the hill, but it is still on the hillside--not in the valley. It's not in the middle, and not on top of the hill either--just down at the bottom.

Beginning Form

1. Pick up your pen and jump ahead. Draw the hill--loop up, down, make a corner, and continue on the line. Overshoot slightly to create a nub on the end.
2. Pick up your pen and jump up to the top. Draw a little hook or tic mark for the serif at the top.
3. Draw the Tower straight down from the serif down to the bottom side of the hill.
4. Jump back to the line, and continue on to the next letter to the left--here represented by a plain bar.

Middle Form

1. You're coming in from the previous letter on the right. Some people stop at the edge of the Taa', while others continue straight on the line up to the front of the hill.
2. Jump or move your pen ahead to the front of the hill. Draw a loop for the hill: up, down, around, and back. Try to come back straight along the line.
3, 4. Continue with the serif and the Tower as with the Beginning Form. Jump to pick up the next letter.

Ending Form

Same as the Middle Form. Remember to leave a small nub at the end, where the hill meets the plain.

Writing Practice

Say the name of the letter, and make its sound,
each time you write the letter.

Writing Practice

Now put them together.
Remember to keep each letter
separate in your mind.

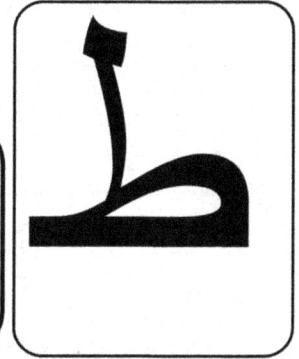

ط	ط	ط	ط

Know The Difference!

Zaa' is just like Taa' except at night, with the evening star Z out over the hill.
You can hear a strong Z sound all around at night.

ظ

Sod is the Sad Sod Sand dune.
It does not have a Tall Tower, but instead is always followed by a short hill-crest.

ص

Dod is just like Sod except it has Dad's Dog on the Dune.
It too has no tower, simply a hill-crest.

ض

Middle Lam has no hill.
It looks like a backwards L.

ـل

Alif also has no hill,
and it is not joined on the left.
It has no bump at the top.

ا

Meem, the Mini Mean Mung bean,
is smaller than the sand dune hill for Taa' and it has no tower.

م

Reading Practice

طِراز

z A R i T
TiRaaz
type; kind; style, model

طِبّ

2 b i T
Tibb
medicine, medical ~

طيب

b y T
Tayyib
O.K.

رَطب

b T a R
RaTb
damp; humid; moist

أطلس

s l T a
aTlas
atlas

بَطاطا

A T A T a b
baTaaTaa
potato

Zaa' (THaa')

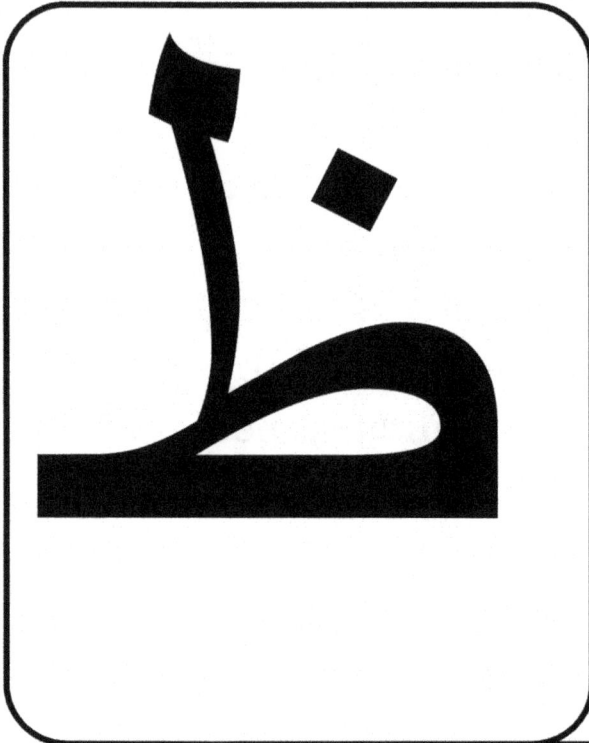

Z

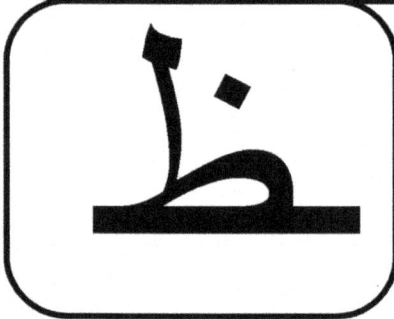 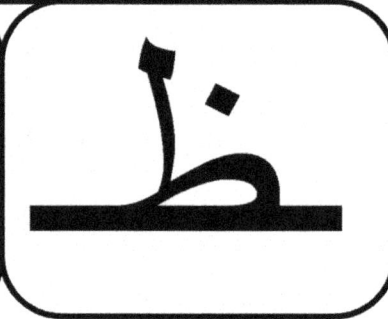 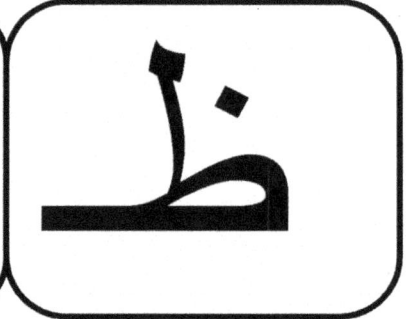

"emphatic voiced alveolar fricative"

ظاء

Zaa' (or spelled THaa', Zoh', or THoh') is called a "strong Z", "dark Z", or "emphatic Z" sound. In most regions, this is actually an "emphatic TH" sound, as in "THat". This is a very strong, buzzing sound, with a hollow, open throat, similar to Dod. The best way to say this sound is to pretend you are a pirate whaler, and say "THarrr she blows!!". When you put lots of grind into the following "Arr", this will automatically open up your throat for the dark emphatic TH. You can also pretend you are a big angel with a deep, open voice, and tell people to "BreaTHe Onnn!". For the Z version, if you say "Brazil" strongly, you might notice how your tongue stays in the back of your mouth, with a hollow behind it. This is a dark Z. You can also say "Zircon" or "Zorro", and pronounce the first syllable like "ZZurrr". This again will open up your throat, and get the strong buzzing sound you need for this letter. Use the TH version for most countries.

Z/TH/6'   *Zaa' CONNECTS on the left.*   Z/ẓ/z̲/DH/Th

Zaa' (THaa')

is the Zircon Z-star by the tower

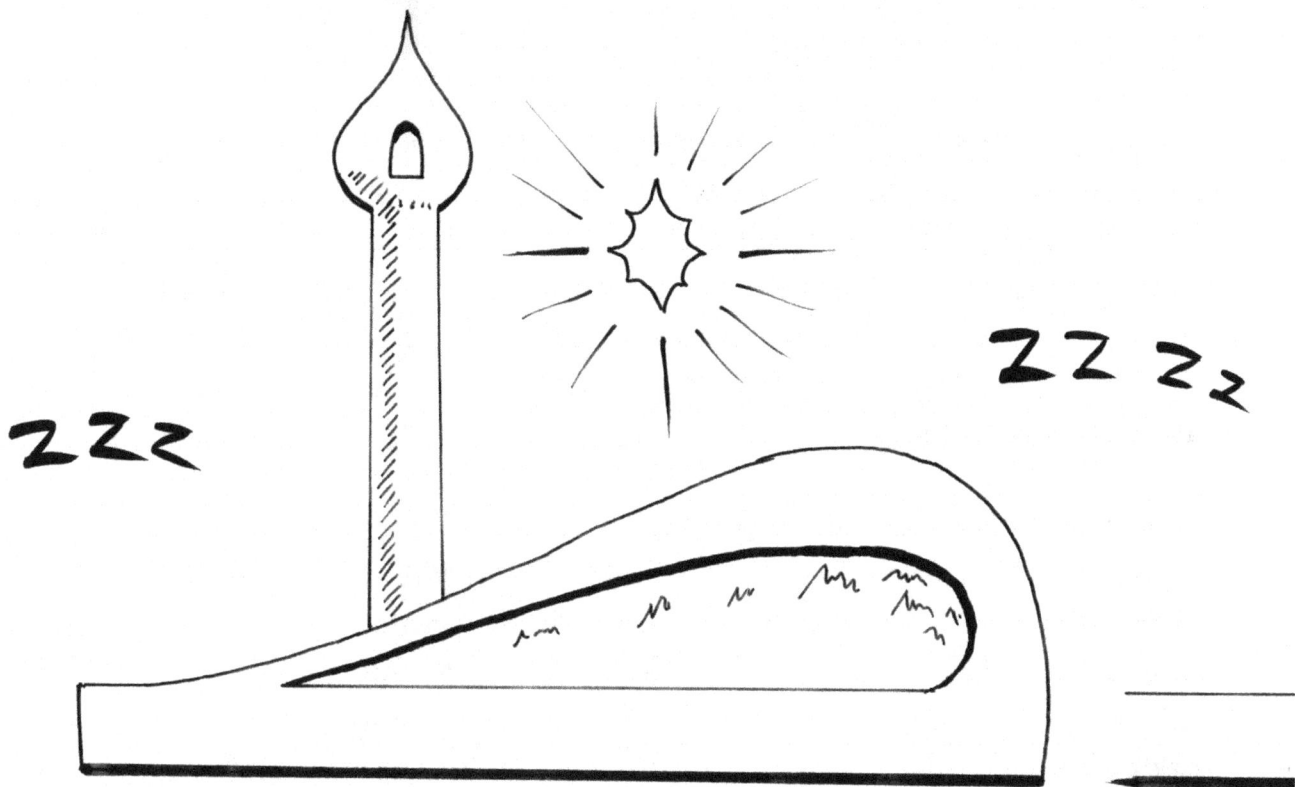

A Strong Z sound
Is being heard all around
As the Zircon star rises
Over the hill.
One *star* by the tower
Gives the dark "Z" power
And that sign, we remember it still.

Helpful Hints

This sound is pronounced with the resonance coming from the back of your open throat. It's different from the light, regular "z" of "zaay", which only comes from the front of the mouth.

The essence of the dark letters is the open throat in the back. This boils down to working with the "aw" sound. Pretend you are Hamlet, giving singing instructions in a dramatic, low, ringing voice. You slowly say, "Drop your Jaw On the Opera Song." Go ahead. Wave your hands dramatically while you do it. And make your throat big and round on the "o" sounds. Take them very slowly, and let them ring.

Now make the e vowel in the "the" in this phrase into another short "o" like the others, kind of like dhaw, but we'll spell it "Tho". Make it hollow. And long. So now you're going to say: "Drop your Jaw On Tho'Opera Song."   Make it even longer. "Drooop your Jawww Onnn Tho'Ooopera Sooong." Keep the "o" hollow, open, and down deep in your throat.

Now simply concentrate on the words in the middle: "OnnTho' ". Run it together. Keep it hollow: "OnnTho'onnTho'onnThonnThonn". Now simply pull out the buzzing Th from the middle: " Tho'. Tho'. " Now make it even shorter. "Th'. Th'. Th'. Th'." Keep the resonance in the back of your throat in your mind while you do this, and your throat will make the right shape--even if you don't say a vowel.

Basically all of the dark sounds in Arabic use this open throat.

Now You Sketch It--Doodles!

How To Write It

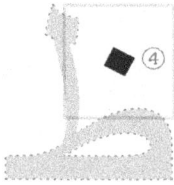

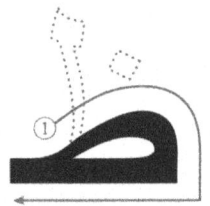

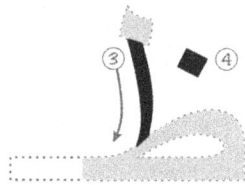

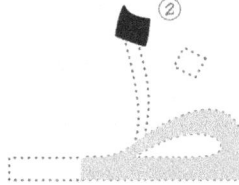

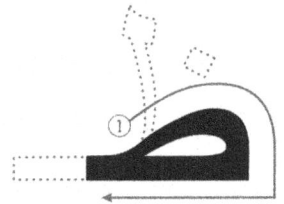

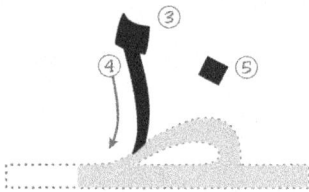

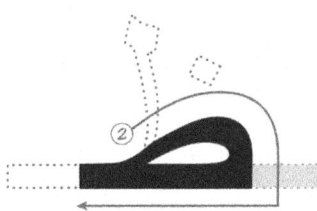

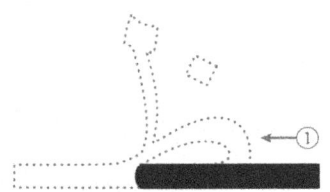

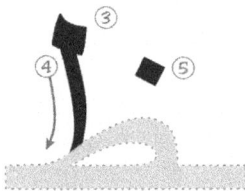

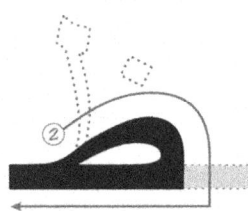

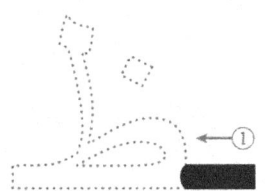

Writing Suggestions

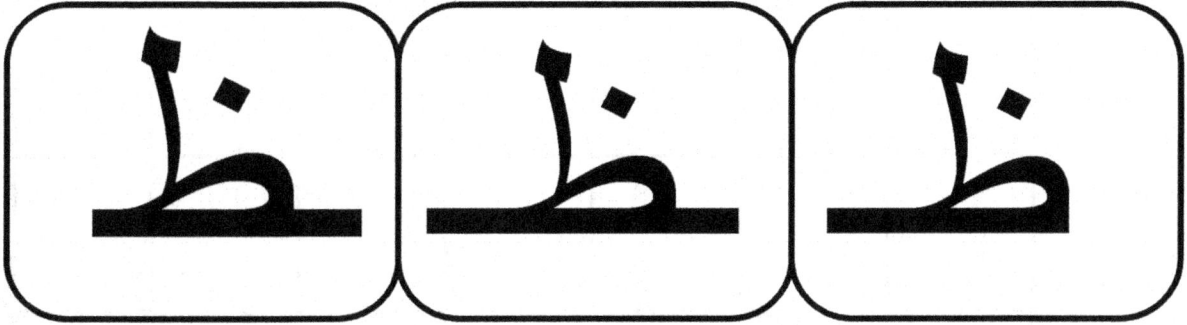

ظ ظ ظ

Stand-Alone Form
1. Pick up your pen and jump ahead. First, draw the hill: Starting on the line, draw a swirling loop back, up, over, and down onto the line. Some people form a hard corner at this point, while others keep the loop going 'round. Now, draw the plain under the hill. Come back flat on the line, cross where you started, and overshoot slightly to form a little nub that sticks out on the left side. The plain goes past the edge of the hill forming a shallow valley, and continues on flat just a bit further.
2. Jump to the top. Put a little tick-mark, hook, or serif up at the top. That's the Torch on the Tower.
3. Now draw a line straight down from the Torch to the bottom side of the hill, just above the valley. That's the Tower.
4. Now you have to indicate that it's a dark night, in order to get the strong Z sound. Put in the Z-star over the hill, it's a simple dot. Make it balanced, so it looks pretty. Put it in the middle of an invisible square! The Z-star should be halfway between the left edge of the Tower, on the left side, and the right edge of the hill, on the right side. We don't want it too close to the tower, and don't stick it too close to the top of the hill, either. From top to bottom, the Z-star is also halfway in the middle, between the top of the Torch on top of the Tower, and the top of the hill.

Beginning Form
1. Pick up your pen and jump ahead. Draw a hill. Overshoot to form a nub at the end.
2, 3. Draw the serif and the Tower.
Jump your pen to the nub at the end of the plain, and continue on drawing the next letter.
4. Come back later and put in the single dot for the Z-star.

Middle Form
1. You're coming in from the previous letter on the right. Some people stop at the edge of the Zaa', while others continue on straight on the line until the base of the hill.
2, 3, 4, 5. Continue on, just as you did with the Beginning Form.

Ending Form
Same as the Middle Form. Leave a nub at the end; the letter does not stop at the bottom of the hill.

Writing Practice

Say the name of the letter, and make its sound,
each time you write the letter.

Writing Practice

Now put them together.
Remember to keep each letter
separate in your mind.

ظ	ظ	ظ	ظ

Know The Difference!

Taa' is just like Zaa except it is the Tall, Tall Tower during the day.

ط

Dod has Dad's Dancing, Dancing Dog on the Dune. The Dune is followed by a short hill-crest. There is no tower.

ض

Sod is the Sad Sod Sand dune all alone by itself. No Z-star, and no tower.

ص

Khaa' is open, not a closed loop, and has no tower beside it.

خ

Final Laam gives a tower, but no hill to the right.

ل

Ghayn is small and triangular, with no following tower.

غ

Reading Practice

حظ

Z H
HaZZ
luck

ظرف

f R Z
ZaRf
adverb; envelope

ظفر

R f Z
ZifR
fingernail;
toenail

أنظر

R Z n u
unZuR
Look!

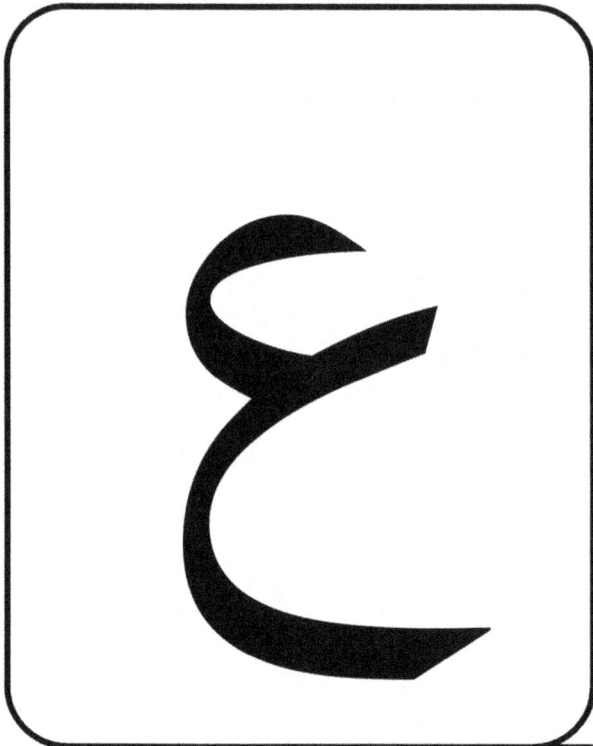

^aein

a

ع

ﻊ ﺤ ﻋ

☾★ *"voiced pharyngeal fricative / epiglottal / pharyngealized glottal stop"* عَين

^aein (^aayn) is a voiced version of Hot Pepper Haa'. It is a soft, strangled "ah" sound, which sounds vaguely like a little lamb bleating. It's also like when the doctor asks you to "Say Ah". To say this, first say "ss-zz-ss-zz-ss-zz" to remind yourself of the difference between voiceless and voiced sounds. Now open your mouth and your throat wide, and say the H in Haa': "HH". This is unvoiced. Now add a voiced "ah" sound into the H. This is your ^a. Go back and forth between "HH-^{aa}-HH-^{aa}" until you can say the "^{aa}" sound whenever you feel like it. ^aein is a DARK consonant.

3 *^aein CONNECTS on the left.* ^a/3/^c/9/ʿ

ᵃein

is the bleating lambs

Three bleating lambs, with ribbons fine
So well behaved, bleat "ᵃein" in line--
The *backwards three*
Sing "Do, Re, Mi"
And huff on bells to make them shine!

Helpful Hints

ᵃein is called "Ayin" in Hebrew. It was originally shaped like an eye ⬭ , but it got turned sideways ߷ and simplified ﻉ .   "ᵃeyn" still means "eye" in Arabic, almost the same as in English.

ᵃein is one of the most interesting letters in the Arabic alphabet. No one knows how to write it in English letters--it seems like everyone tries to make up their own sign. The most popular methods are a raised superscript "a" (ᵃ), a "3", or a raised superscript "c" (ᶜ). Other people use a superscript "9" (⁹) or a backquote (`). Your English textbook may be different yet.

ᵃein has four different forms. The Stand-Alone Form is very fancy--it looks like a hooded cape, or a shepard's crook. It takes the form of a "backwards three".   However, the Beginning Form only echos the hood on the cape--it looks like a singing lamb's mouth, or maybe a cᵃn-opener.
The Middle Form looks like a little triangular bell with a blue ribbon attached to it. And the Ending Form also looks like a little bell, with a long ribbon that looks like a sitting lamb.

ᵃein is also one of the most interesting letters to learn how to pronounce. You really need to hear this from a native speaker in order to recognize it and understand how it sounds. And then you can start to experiment with how you can make this sound yourself, with your own throat.

Here are some exercises that might help:

Loosen up by first doing an imitation of a big, fat lamb bleating:
"Beaᵃeaᵃeaᵃeaᵃea! Beaᵃeaᵃeaᵃeaᵃea! Beaᵃeaᵃeaᵃeaᵃea!"
Notice how the sound comes from the back of the throat, which is tight. There are grinding clicks in the middle, where the sound gets blocked instantaneously by the bottom of the throat, but it's still coming out. We want to be able to capture one of those quick grinding clicks for the ᵃein.

Sing the lowest note that you can possibly reach, with an "Aaaah". Now sing one note lower.

Pretend that you are huffing on your glasses, or huffing on a brass bell, in order to start shining it up. But use your voice while you're huffing--don't keep it silent. Go "Hᵃᵃᵃᵃᵃᵃᵃᵃᵃh! Hᵃᵃᵃᵃᵃᵃᵃᵃᵃᵃᵃh!"

Pretend that a doctor is sticking a tongue-depressor down your throat. Stick out your tongue, open your throat and say "Aaah" in a strangled way with lots of scrape.

Touch the lowest part of your tongue possible against the back of your throat, as if choking.

Say "Aaah!" like Dr. Stephen Hawkings's robot voice synthesizer.

Make the sound of a car engine trying unsuccessfully to start without any gas in the tank.

Think of when you're totally disgusted by something gross. You say "Eeeeew!" with lots of grind.

University teacher Sarah Ouwayda suggests "Think about saying a silent 'ah' in your mind, but connect it to the next letter *without stopping*. If you stop, it's a hamza."

Now You Sketch It--Doodles!

How To Write It

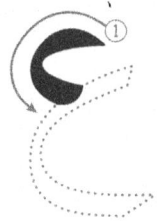

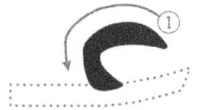

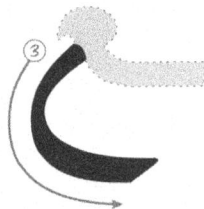

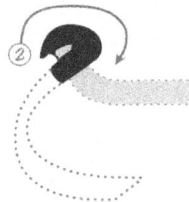

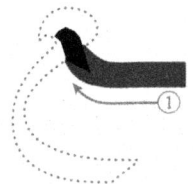

88

Writing Suggestions

Stand-Alone Form

1. Start a quarter of the way above the line. Draw a small open "c" red-riding-hood shape down onto the line.
2. Now draw another "C" shape that is twice as large, underneath and touching it. This stretches almost completely below the line, except for the top part. This is the shepherd's cloak. The left edge of the hood and the cloak are in line--but because the cloak is twice as large, the right edge has to start much further in front.

Beginning Form

1. Echo the red-riding-hood shape. Start a quarter of the way above the line. Draw a small, open "c" shape down onto the line. It looks like the top part of a can-opener, or a little lamb's mouth singing.
2. Starting just slightly above the line, draw a straight line down to the line. Meet and cross the end of the previous stroke. Continue on the line on to the next letter.

Middle Form

1. You're coming along the line from the previous character. Take a slight corner and go up slightly.
2. A second stroke starts here. In the old days, people would lift the pen and start a new stroke. Now people mostly just keep going, and make a tiny corner. Anyway, make a tiny hook or a crook that starts on the left, loops over the top in a flat manner, has a rounded corner on the right side, and then crooks in to go back down to the line. The whole thing forms a tiny loop that should be a little flattened--it should look like an upside-down triangle. This is the bell, or the bow-knot in the ribbon.
3. Continue on the line, on to the next letter. This is the lamb's ribbon.

Ending Form

1. You're coming along the line, in from the previous character. Take a slight corner and go up slightly.
2. The second stroke is the hook or crook to make the rest of the bell or the bow-knot. It's slightly higher and tighter than the Middle Form version. Many people don't bother with flattening the top like a triangle, and just make the whole thing a tiny round loop. This is the sitting lamb's bell.
3. The ending stroke is larger and more ornate on the ending form. It curves in, underneath. It hangs down about two-thirds of the way below the line, and ends up pointing backwards, like the cloak.

Writing Practice

Say the name of the letter, and make its sound,
each time you write the letter.

Writing Practice

Now put them together.
Remember to keep each letter
separate in your mind.

ع	عـ	ـعـ	ـح

Know The Difference!

Ghein is just like ªein except it always has a single dot at the top. That's the Paris Root Beer bottle.

غ غ غ
ـغ ـغ ـغ

Haa' has a Hot Hat
on top of a big, open-mouth curve.

ح

Meem in the middle, the Mini Mean Mung bean, has a loop that is round and bean-shaped. Ending Meem has a root that points straight down.

ـم م

Beginning haa' has a loop but it has a Heroic cape above it. Middle haa' looks like a small Hummingbird.

ـه هـ

Haa' at the beginning or middle opens to the left. It's Hot Pepper Harry's Hot Pepper. HHHot!

حـ حـ

Wow the Wide White toWel
has a loop but curves off to the left, not open to the right.

و

Reading Practice

مَعَ

a ᵃ a m
maᵃa
with

بَعد

d ᵃ a b
baᵃd
yet, not yet

بَعض

D ᵃ a b
baᵃD
some

عاج

j A ᵃ
ᵃaaj
ivory

جامِع

ᵃ i m A j
jaamiᵃ
mosque

نَعَم

m a ᵃ a n
naᵃam
Yes

عِنَب

b a n i ᵃ
ᵃinab
raisins

عَفواً

an w f a ᵃ
ᵃafwan
Excuse me!; Sorry!;
You're welcome

93

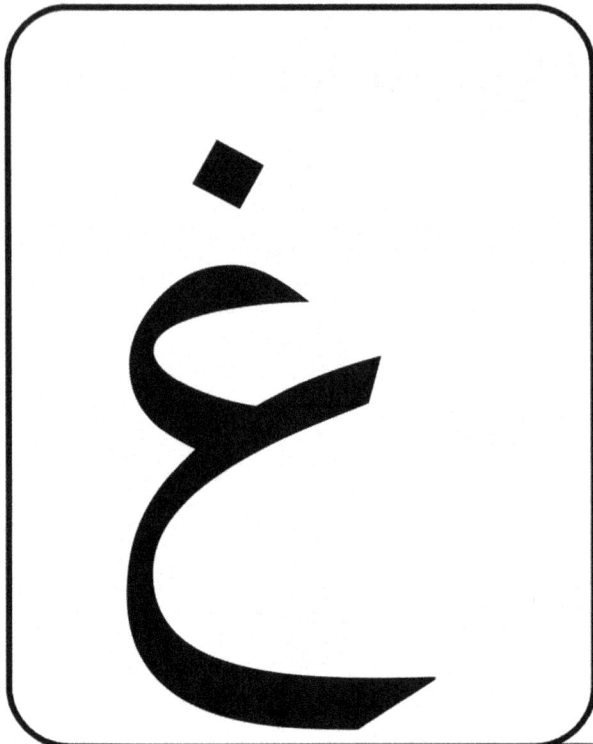

ghein

gh

غ غ

غ غـ ـغـ ـغ

"voiced velar fricative"

غَين

ghein (ghayn) is a voiced version of Khubla Khan Bach's "Kh". It is basically the sound that you make in the back of your throat when you gargle with mouthwash. It is also close to the throaty rolled, scraping "r" sound you get if you ask a friend from Paris to say "Paris root beer". It also sounds like a motorboat motor imitation: "gh-gh-gh". Start by saying "kk-gg-kk-gg" to remind yourself of the difference between voiceless and voiced. Now move the sound to the back of your tongue. Say "kh-gh-kh-gh". Besides scraping, the sound will roll or trill by itself. Practice until you can say "gh" by itself any time you want to.

gh / 3'   *Ghein CONNECTS on the left.*   gh/gh

ghein

is gargling with Paris Root Beer

Three lambs, while on a motor-boat,
Must gargle for their poor sore throats.
Along the *Rhein*
In style they dine
And purr with Paris Root-Beer notes!

Helpful Hints

The letter ghein looks just like the letter ªein with an extra dot, being the bottle of Paris root beer, balanced on top.
The sounds themselves are different, though. Although they are both voiced trills that come from the back of the throat, the ghein is a closed, rolled "r" or "g" sound that comes from hitting the back of your tongue against the far back of your mouth. Whereas the ªein is a choking click that comes from the very bottom of the throat, almost the top of the chest.

Ghein is almost similar to a cat's purr. The throat is trilling. The same trill is also used when making the *coo* of a dove, except of course it's much higher in pitch.
Stick with the mouthwash gargle sound for ghein.

People also usually want to know the difference between Raa' and ghein.

Raa' is similar to a Spanish rolled rr. The front tip of your tongue bounces against the top of the roof of your mouth in front. Your tongue is doing the vibrating.

Ghein, on the other hand, is similar to a Paris French r.
It comes completely from the back of the throat, at the bottom. Although the back bottom of your tongue is hitting the back of your throat, as when you gargle, it almost feels like your whole throat is vibrating.

Now You Sketch It--Doodles!

How To Write It

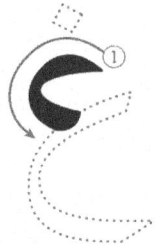

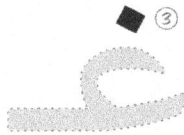

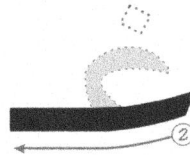

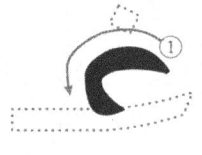

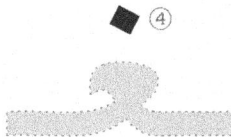

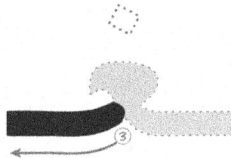

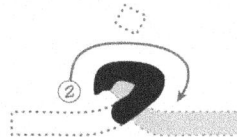

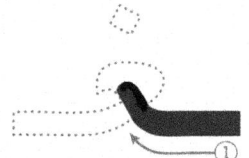

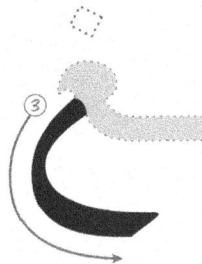

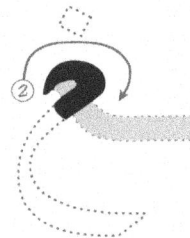

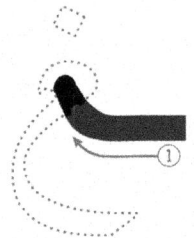

ع

غ

ج

ح

Writing Suggestions

غـ   ـغـ   ـغ

Stand-Alone Form
1. Start slightly above the line. Make a looping hook that looks like a red-riding-hood on down to touching the line.
2. Start on or right above the line. Make a bigger cape shape. The left sides line up. The right side is slightly in front of the hood.
3. Put a dot centered above the hood. That's the Paris Root Beer.

Beginning Form
1. Draw an open-mouth can-opener hook down onto the line.
2. Starting slightly in front and just slightly above, draw a straight line that comes down to the line & continues on to the next letter.
3. Come back later and add the gargle bottle of Root Beer on top.

Middle Form
1. Come in on the line, and then go up slightly.
2,3. Jog your pen, and start a flat hook that goes over, down, around.
4. Come back sometime later to put the gargle bottle over the top.

Ending Form
1. Come in on the line, and up.
2. Jog your pen and make a flat-topped loop. Go around, over, down.
3. Continue on and make a big swish for the sitting lamb at the end.
4. Now put the dot centered over the loop for the Paris Root Beer.

Writing Practice

Say the name of the letter, and make its sound,
each time you write the letter.

Writing Practice

Now put them together.
Remember to keep each letter
separate in your mind.

غـ	ـغـ	ـغـ	غ

Know The Difference!

ᵃein is just like ghein except it has no dots. It is just the singing lambs by themselves, without the Paris Root Beer bottles.	ع عـ ـعـ ـع
Fat Freddy Faa' has a loop that is flat on the right, not triangular and flat on top.	فـ ف
Khubla Khan's Khap is shaped like a Mongolian helmet with a spike on top. It opens to the left.	خـ ـخـ ـخ
haa' loops like a Heroic cape or a small Hummingbird. It has no dot over it.	هـ ـه
Meem has a loop at the end, but has a Mini Mean Mung bean tap root pointing down. It also has no dot on top.	م مـ ـم
Dod has Dad's Dancing, Dancing Dog on the Dune. The sand Dune is a closed loop.	ضـ ـض

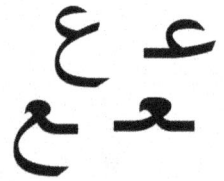

Reading Practice

غَير

r y a gh
ghayr
other

غرب

b r gh
gharb
west

غاز

z A gh
ghaaz
gas

غُبار

r A b u gh
ghubaar
dust

غِطاء

' A T i gh
ghiTaa'
lid; bedsheet

غير حاد

d A H r y gh
ghayr Haadd
Not So Spicy, "Mild"

Bonus Marks

Here are your four extra-credit bonus marks for this volume. Again, these marks are not "real letters" and do not go into the alphabetic order. Rather, they are marks that ride above or beneath the other letters in the word. They add extra information to the word and its pronunciation. Most of these here are grammar markers that help determine how the word is used in a sentence. Don't worry about that for now...just learn how to write them and pronounce them.

You're about to see and get a feel for three doubled short vowels ending in N, plus one important extra sign that means no vowel at all. What?
You'll see in just a bit.

A Word on Nunnation
(called "tanween" in Arabic)

There are three irregular variations on the basic short vowels that we learned in the previous book. These are:
fat-Ha-tein, kasRa-tein, and Dom-ma-tein.

Each of these variations only appears at the **end** of a word.

Each of these variations is written by doubling the sign.
Fat-Ha-tein and kasRa-tein are obvious, as you'll see. Dom-ma-tein used to be written with two Dom-mahs a long time ago, but people got lazy, so the second one is just sketched out.

Each of these variations is pronounced by adding an extra "n" at the end of the vowel. This is included in the -tein mark for free, it does *not* need you to draw a Noon letter "n" after the word (we'll be covering the letter Noon in the third book).
Your teacher will tell you this is called "nunnation". No, it does not mean adding a nation of nuns to every word that you pronounce. That would be a terrible habit. "Nunnation" is a fancy technical word that simply means "adding an 'N' onto the end of what you're saying". They couldn't think how to spell "N" properly in a word ("N-nation? En-nation?"), so they just turned it into "nun". It's in the English dictionary. Honest.

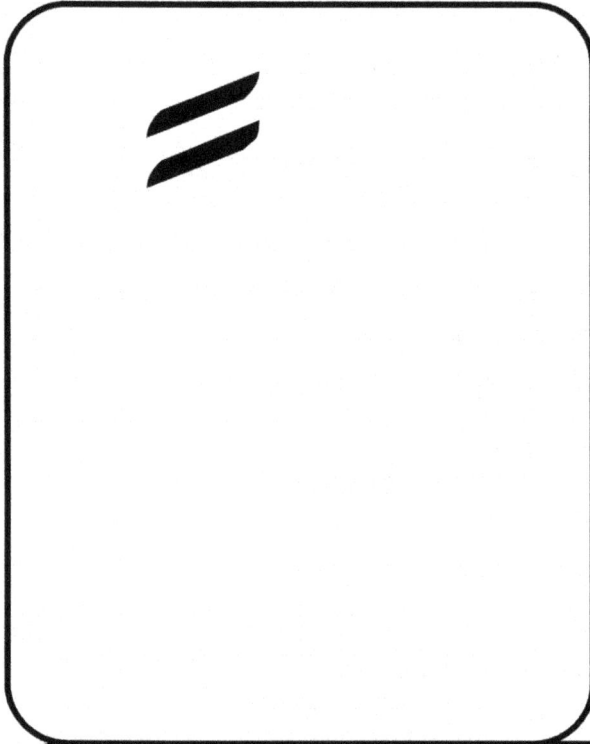

fat-Ha-tein

an

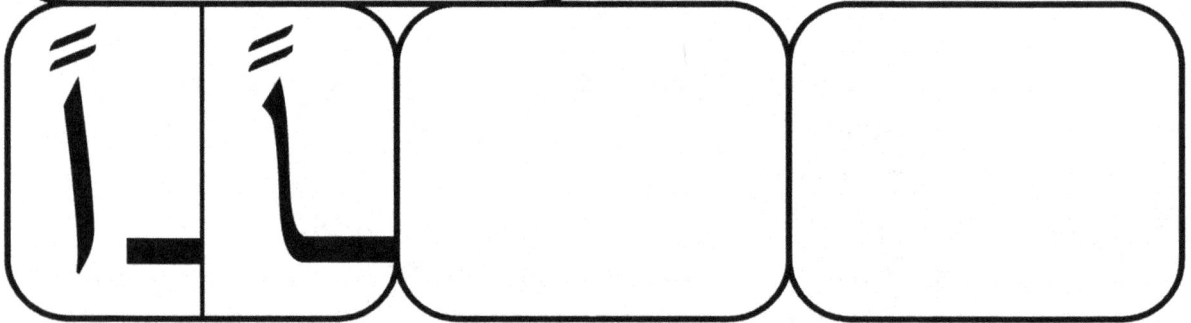

"short low back vowel with nunnation"

فَتْحَتَين

Fat-Ha-tein (or spelled fatHatain or fatHatayn), the "twin fat-Ha's", only comes at the end of a word. It is pronounced just like a fat-Ha that ends in N: "an".

an

an

fatHatein

is two twin fat High tiny eyebrows raised at the end

Father Tine

holds up a silent finger and
raises TWO tiny eyebrows,
mumbles '...ann" softly,
and *that's final.*

Helpful Hints

Fat-Ha-tein is drawn by writing two fat-Ha's, one on top of the other, at the end of a word.

Fat-Ha-tein is used for turning words into adverbs, just like "ly" is used in English. If you quietly and carefully think about how you do actions, you will rapidly understand this. So it is an ending having to do with grammar.

Unfortunately, fat-Ha-tein is *irregular*. You would think that it could simply be drawn over the last letter in the word, like kasRa-tein and Dom-ma-tein are. There should be no problems, right?

But such is not the case. Almost always, the fat-Ha-tein needs to be drawn riding on top of a "ghost 'Aalif". It's like Father Tine's finger pointing up to the fat-Ha-tein, to emphasize that it's an extra syllable coming as the ending.

The "ghost 'Aalif" is **not pronounced**. It's because it's *not really there*. It is a lot like the "ghost u" that has to follow a "q" in English. Why do we write "quick" instead of "qick"? It just has to be there in order to look good. So it's the same way with the "ghost 'Aalif" under the fat-Ha-tein. It has to be there, in order to give the fat-Ha-tein something to "ride on" at the end.

Because the ghost 'Aalif comes at the end, it will be drawn in two different ways. If the previous letter is an <u>unconnected</u> letter, the 'Aalif will be drawn as a single stroke straight down, like a Stand-Alone 'Aalif. And, if the previous letter is a <u>connected</u> letter, it will be drawn as an Ending 'Aalif, with the line curving into a single stroke going straight up.

For later reference, the fat-Ha-tein does not need a ghost 'Aalif if it is coming over a taa'-marbuuTa sign or a full-sized hamza at the end. It's because these are already special endings themselves. We'll be covering these later on at the end of the third book, so don't worry about them right now.

Now You Sketch It--Doodles!

How To Write It

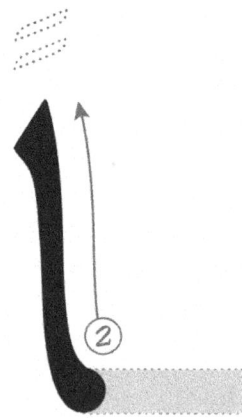

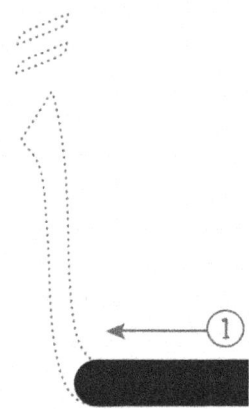

Writing Suggestions

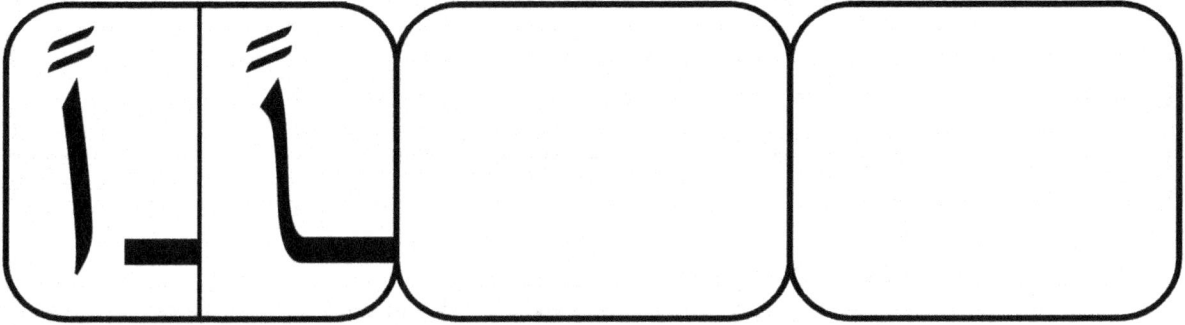

Stand-Alone Form

Technically, there is not a Stand-Alone Form for fatHatein. However, the simple symbol is drawn with two FatHa, two diagonal strokes, one on top of the other. The fat-Ha-tein sign only appears at the *end* of words.

Beginning Form, Middle Form

There is no Beginning Form, and no Middle Form. Don't you like letters like these?

Ending Form, Previous Letter Unconnected

1. The Ending Form of FatHatein consists of two FatHa, two diagonal strokes, one on top of the other. However, unless the last letter is something like a taa-marbuTaa or a large hamza, the FatHatein requires a "ghost 'Aalif" to ride on. If the last letter in the word is an UNCONNECTED letter, the 'Aalif takes the Stand-Alone Form. Start by drawing a Stand-Alone 'Aalif as a single large stroke from all the way up, down to the line.
2, 3. Fill in the fatHatein strokes on top of the 'Aalif. Because they are on top of the tall 'Aalif, they will float significantly above the line of text--sometimes almost up into the previous line of text. Leave a small space above the 'Aalif to the slashes.

Ending Form, Previous Letter Connected

1. If the previous letter is CONNECTED, the ghost 'Aalif is the Ending Form. Come in on the line from the previous letter.
2. The Ending 'Aalif goes *upwards* from the line to the full height. Point it up, not out.
3. 4. Fill in the fatHatein tiny slashes on top of the 'Aalif. Leave a small space between the top of the 'Aalif and the slashes. Keep them stacked straight on top.

Writing Practice

Say the name of the letter, and make its sound,
each time you write the letter.

Writing Practice

It doesn't make any sense to practice writing these connected together,
because there are no Beginning nor Middle forms.
Please use the space to practice words your instructor gives you,
or you may copy words from
the Reading Practice on the following page.

أ ـأ

Know The Difference!

Fat-Ha has only a single slash, and can appear anywhere in the word, not just at the end.

Kasra-tein has two slashes, but only appears *below* the line.

Hamza is rounded and is all one piece. It looks like a little letter "c" (that's the hamster) on top of its surf-board. Sometimes in handwriting the two slashes of a fatHatein will connect in an angular backwards "z" shape, not round, so you have to be careful. These are very different in print, though.

"Double Quotes" are vertical. They start and end outside the letters of a word, not on top of the end letter.

One style of a hand-drawn Dom-mah-tein can look an awful lot like a fat-Ha-tein, except it has rounded hooks at the ends. You might have to get this one from context.

taa-marbuuta has a crown that is two dots, not two slashes.

Reading Practice

غَدَاً

Aan d a gh
ghadan
tomorrow

جدّاً

Aan 2 d j
jid-dan
very

أَيضاً

Aan D y a'
'ayDan
also

طبعاً

Aan ª b T
Tabªan
Of course! Certainly!

عَفواً

Aan w f a ª
ªafwan
You're Welcome!

شُكراً

Aan R k u sh
shukRan
Thank You!

مَساءً

'an A s a m
masaa'an
in the evening

قليلاً

LAan y l a Q
Qaleelan
a little

115

kasRa-tein

in

in

"short high front vowel with nunnation"

گَسرَتَین

KasRa-tein (or spelled "kasratayn"), the "twin kasRas",
only comes at the end of words.
It is pronounced just like a kasRa that ends in N: "in".
Sometimes this can been closer to "een" or "en".

in   in

116

kasRatein

is twin casserole fish in a tin

Final Fin
beneath the sea
Fishes Twin
Are happy free

At last they're in
Together now
Enjoying ten
Good endings now.

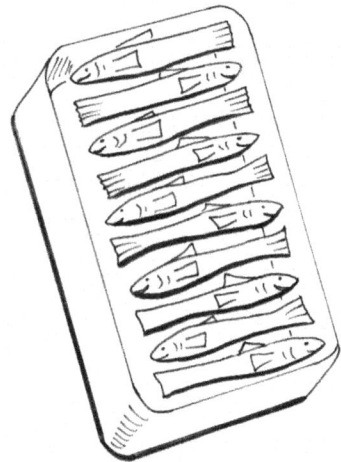

Ten in the tin
at the end.

Helpful Hints

KasRa-tein is the second twinned short vowel with nunnation. It also *only* appears at the *end* of words, so you don't need to worry about what it looks like in the middle or at the beginning. It also has nunnation--it's pronounced like a regular kasRa that ends in "n". And it's drawn with a doubled kasRa, two strokes.

Unlike the irregular fatHa-tein, kasRa-tein does *not* need a "ghost 'Aalif" or any other special letter to ride on. It simply comes at the end of the regular word, with nothing else extra added except its two slashes.

The name "kasRa-tein" rhymes with "Einstein". (Although "kasRa-tein" looks like it should end in a kasRa-tein, in actuality you'll notice that it's spelled ending with a Yaa and a Noon.)

Now You Sketch It--Doodles!

How To Write It

Writing Suggestions

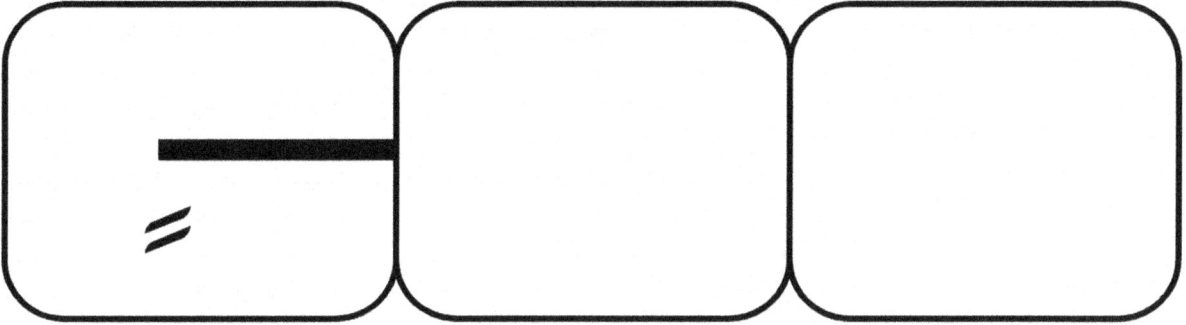

Stand-Alone Form
Technically there is no stand-alone form for this sign, unless you're talking about the letter itself. See the Ending Form.

Beginning Form
There is no Beginning Form.

Middle Form
There is no middle form, either. This makes up for having to learn ªein and ghein in this book. You've earned your vacation.

Ending Form
The ending form for kasra-tain is embarrassingly simple. Simply draw two kasras, two diagonal marks, one under the other, at the end of the word under the end of the last letter.

Writing Practice

Say the name of the letter, and make its sound,
each time you write the letter.

Writing Practice

It doesn't make any sense to practice writing these connected together,
because there are no Beginning nor Middle forms.
Please use the space to practice words your instructor gives you,
or you may copy words from
the Reading Practice on the following page.

Know The Difference!

kasRah is only a single slash. It can appear anywhere in the word, not just at the end.	ِ
fat-Ha-tein always appears riding ON TOP of the last letter--which is usually a "ghost 'Aalif".	ً
hamza rides on the bottom of an 'Aalif in order to indicate a kasRah. hamza comes in only one piece, and it's rounded.	إ
Double Quotes are vertical and ride above, beside the letters, not on top of them nor underneath.	"
The two dots are the skate wheels for the Yippee Snakes on Roller Skates Ending yaa'. They come below at the end, but are part of the letter. And they're dots, not slashes.	ي
Beginning yaa' or middle yaa' also each have two dots, not slashes.	يـ ـيـ

Reading Practice

راعٍ

in ^a A R

Raa^ain

patron; sponsor;
cowboy; shepherd

خالٍ

in l A kh

khaalin

empty, bare

ضَواحٍ

in H A w a D

DawaaHin

suburbs

راقٍ

in Q A R

RaaQin

high-class, posh

Dom-ma-tein

ضٍ

un

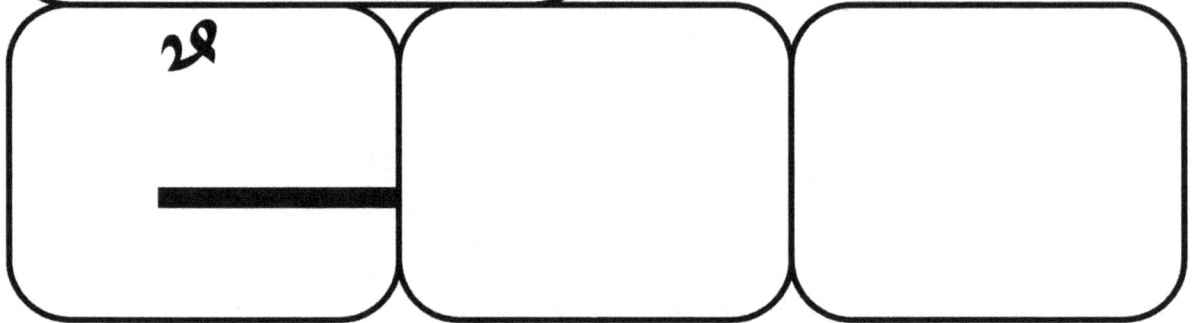

"short high back vowel with nunnation"

ضَمَّتَين

Dom-ma-tein, the "twin Dom-mas", only comes at the end of words. It is pronounced just like a Dom-mah that ends in N: "oon" or "on", like the last sound in "spoon", "fortune", "Houston", or "mastodon". The vowel sound is usually closest to the short "oo" found in "good", with an N on the end.

un   un

Dom-ma-tein

is the Ruined Spoon of Brigadoon

oon!
oon!
oon!

I say--Good Fortune!

The Ruined Spoon of Brigadoon
Bent by a loony dune baboon!
The oo - n sign
Is "Dom-ma-tein"
So croon a noon-moon, June spoon tune!

Helpful Hints

Dom-ma-tein is drawn like someone was going to draw
two Dom-mahs, but they got tired halfway through the second one
and just stopped. Just remember it has the ruined spoon shape--
--the handle of the spoon has been bent.

A Dom-ma-tein in *print* for the newspapers and the signs, which is
what we are learning, can be different from a *handwritten*
Dom-ma-tein. The handwritten version can look like the printed
version; two Dom-mahs side by side; one Dom-mah upside-down
on top of another; or two curves that look like Dom-mahs.
This can make some handwriting intertesting to read. You should
stick with the version that looks like the printed typeface yourself.

Dom-ma-tein always comes at the end, and it always floats above
the last letter, on top of the line. Unlike the irregular fat-Ha-tein,
Dom-ma-tein does not need any extra letters drawn in to ride on.
Just put it above the last letter like normal.

Dom-ma-tein's pronunciation can be interesting as well. It is a lot
like our word "fortune". What kind of vowel is that in the second
syllable? Well, it's spelled "tune", and technically it is probably
supposed to be a "long oo" to rhyme with "spoon" or "goose".
But in actuality, most people are brought up pronouncing it with a
"short oo", to sound like "good", "woman", or "cushion". But it
could even be pronounced with a "short u" to rhyme with "fun".
It seems they are all so close there is almost no difference.
Dom-ma-tein is almost the same. Try sticking with the "short oo"
version ("good") until you hear the people around you speaking.

Now You Sketch It--Doodles!

How To Write It

Handwritten Forms

Writing Suggestions

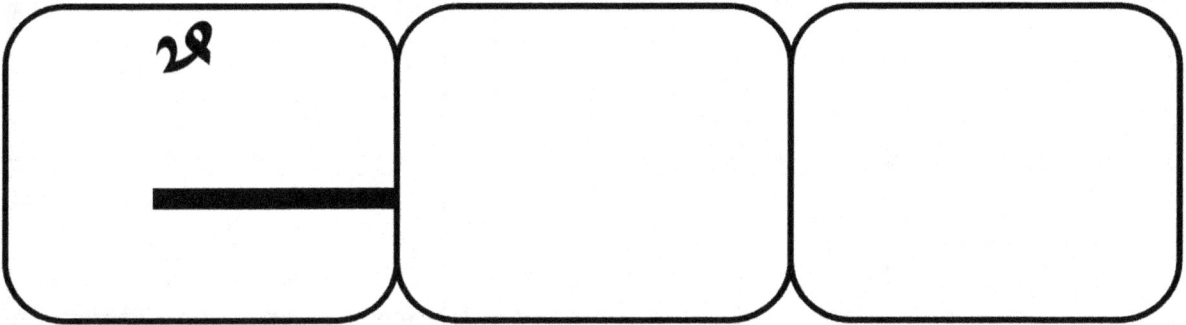

Stand-Alone Form
Dom-ma-tein is a small sign that comes at the end of a word.
It floats above the last letter, just like other vowel signs do.
Because of this, there is no stand-alone form, unless you're talking
about the letter itself. The Dom-ma-tein sign is a grammatical ending
meaning "a", and it *only* appears above the last letter in a word.

Beginning Form
There is no Beginning Form.

Middle Form
Yes, that's right. There is no Middle Form, either.

Ending Form
1. Start above the letter. Starting at the lower right, draw a loop clock-
   wise up, around over the top, and down. Leave a tiny stem sticking
   out on the lower right. The entire loop is very small.
2. Continuing on straight without picking up your pen, draw a slightly
   curved tiny line at about 30 degrees hanging down to the left. That's
   the straight part of the spoon handle.
3. Now draw an open hook counter-clockwise. The hook should be
   about the same size as the first loop. That's the bent spoon handle.

Writing Practice

Say the name of the letter, and make its sound,
each time you write the letter.

Writing Practice

It doesn't make any sense to practice writing these connected together,
because there are no Beginning nor Middle forms.
Please use the space to practice words your instructor gives you,
or you may copy words from
the Reading Practice on the following page.

Know The Difference!

Regular Dom-mah only has a single loop. It does not have the ruined bent spoon handle.	ۈ
fat-Ha-tein is two slashes. No loop.	⸗
Regular fat-Ha is only a single slash, very simple.	◌َ
hamza the surfing hamster is open to the right. There is no closed loop. The hamster is on top of the surf-board. It is different from Dom-ma-tein's ruined spoon handle, which is underneath, opening to the left.	ء
Qof is much larger. It sits on the line, hanging down under, and has a crown of two dots on top.	ق
Wow also is a large, full-sized letter, and sits on the line, hanging below. It has no ruined spoon handle.	و

Reading Practice

كِتَابٌ

un b A t i k
kitaabun
a book

كَلبٌ

un b l a k
kalbun
a dog

بَيتٌ

un t y a b
baytun
a house

حِصانٌ

un n A S i H
HiSaanun
a horse

sukoon

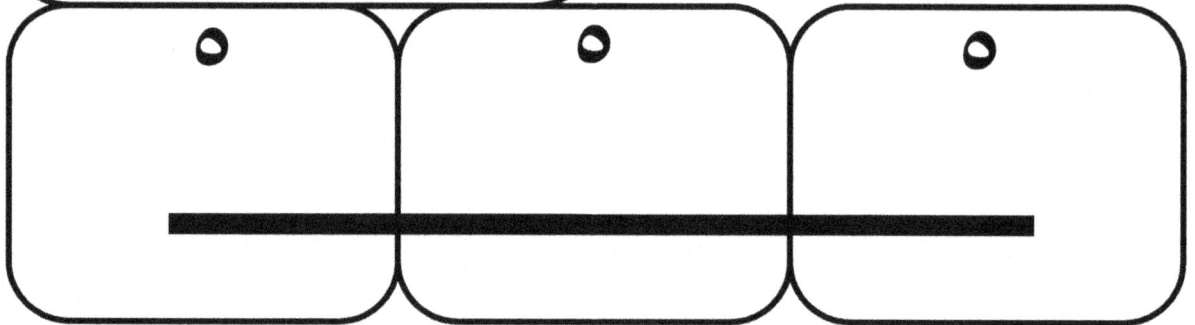

سُكون

sukoon (or sukuun) is a sign for "no vowel when you might expect one". It thus fills the same role as the English apostrophe in words like "can't" and "I'm". But we're already using the apostrophe for the hamza, and English doesn't have any problem with consonants running together. So we simply don't write the sukoon at all when we're writing down the Arabic using Roman letters. Also it is just a spelling mark and has no sound, so there's no pronunciation to learn. What an easy symbol!

sukoon

is a zero sun

A tiny sun
Is called "sukoon"
And it means there's no
following vowel there.

Two consonants together
It's easy to know whether
Vowels come, or none will run,
just see sukoon.

Helpful Hints

Sukuun looks a little like a tiny **zero**,
which is helpful in remembering that it means that an
expected vowel is missing.

In Arabic, each consonant is "supposed" to have a vowel
after it. So when you see two consonants in a row, you
know that you're supposed to put in a fat-Ha, a kasRa, or a
Dom-mah when you **say** the word--even if they're not
written in. Because, the short vowels are allowed to be
skipped--they're allowed to be *not written down* for most
normal writing for adults. It's a little like when we skip
writing the "o" in "can't". Everyone understands it actually
means "cannot"--it's just faster to write it that way,
leaving the "o" out.

But what happens when the writer really <u>did</u> want two
consonants to come together without a vowel?
For example, "dars" (دَرْس) meaning "lesson"?

In this case, a sukuun should be put over the first consonant
in place of the missing vowel mark.

However, in practice, the sukuun is often left out of most
everyday writing, unless it is truly required. As in English,
which word is meant is understood from the context of the
words around it.

Now You Sketch It--Doodles!

How To Write It

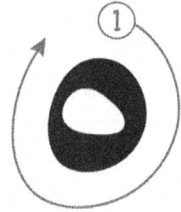

Writing Suggestions

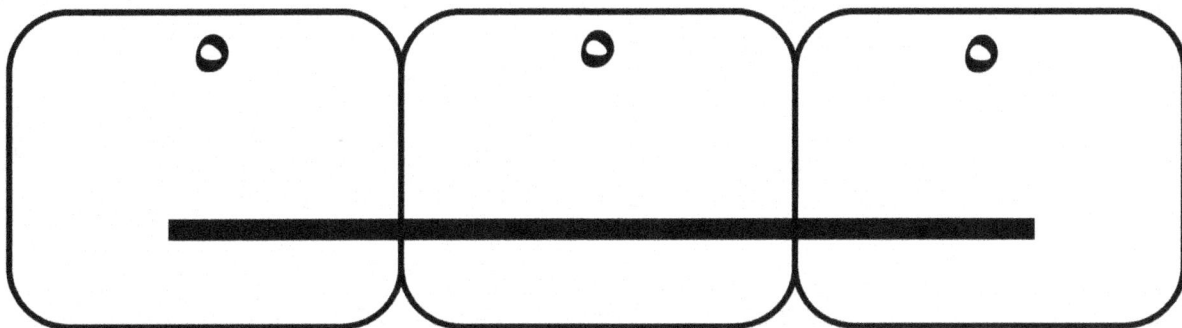

Stand-Alone Form

1. Sukoon is a mark that only appears above a consonant to indicate that there's no following vowel. So it doesn't really have a Stand-Alone Form, except if you're talking about the letter itself. Anyway, sukoon is drawn like a tiny letter "o"--very close to our "degrees" symbol used to indicate temperature for the weather. Make it round, and make sure it closes. It floats above and slightly to the left of its base.

Beginning Form

1. Sukoon slightly follows the consonant that it is over. It is always drawn above, never below. Even at the beginning of words, which is extremely rare, the sukoon is going to be above the first consonant. It does not make sense for a sukoon to start a word by itself--it has to be based on a consonant. Draw the sukoon using a tiny circle.

Middle Form
Same.

Ending Form
Same.

Writing Practice

Say the name of the letter, and make its sound,
each time you write the letter.

Writing Practice

It doesn't make much sense to practice writing these connected together,
because sukuun is simply a spelling mark that goes over other letters.
Please use the space to practice words your instructor gives you,
or you may copy words from
the Reading Practice on the following page.

Know The Difference!

Dom-mah looks like a loop of blue wool. It has a little thread hanging down from the left. It is shaped more like a loop, with a corner at the bottom, and does not look like a completely round circle.	ۈ
Dom-ma-tein, the Ruined Spoon, looks like a spoon that got bent by a looney baboon. It has the bent spoon handle, and again does not look like a completely round circle. Lots of extra parts.	ۉ
hamza also rides above letters on top of the line. However, it is a slightly larger open curve, not completely closed. Also, it has a little flat line down at the bottom; that's the hamster's surfboard.	ء
Shad-dah consists of two loops, and they're both open at the top.	ش
haa' is a complete loop, but it is a full-sized letter. It's much larger than sukuun. It sits on the line, so it does not ride up above the other letters as a mark. And it has a single corner at the top--it's not completely round.	ه
Beginning meem is also a real, full-sized letter. It sits on the line, not above other letters. And it has a mung bean-sprout tail coming out of the left side.	م

Reading Practice

أَكَلَة

ah a l a k a
akalaah
eaters

أَكْلَه

h a l * k a
aklah
meal, fruit

تَيَّتَ

a t a 2 y a b
bay-yata
to put away

بَيْتْ

* t * y a b
bayt
house

شَكَلَ

a l a k a sh
shakala
hang up

شكْل

l * k a sh
shakl
shape; which kind

قَتَل

l a t a Q
Qatal
he killed

قَتْل

l * t a Q
Qatl
killing

Congratulations!

You have faithfully completed all of the exercises in the book. You are now a new person!

"The mind, once expanded to the dimensions
of larger ideas, never returns to its original size."
Oliver Wendell Holmes

To certify your accomplishment, we are here including a "Certificate of Completion" for you.

If you have an instructor, or if there is someone else who is teaching the course for you, you can have them sign your certificate for you.

If you're teaching the course to yourself, sign the certificate yourself after you've completed all the exercises and you know you deserve it.

Why not carefully tear your certificate out of the book, and post it on the wall where you can see it. It will remind you to be proud of your accomplishments. This will help focus your mind, so that you will become even stronger and more successful. Go for it!!

Certificate of Completion

This is to certify that

_____

has successfully completed

Week 2

Actually Learn Arabic Letters

and is fully entitled to receive all the benefits thereof
from this day onward
all through life.

Awarded this day

_____
date of achievement

_____
Signatory Authority

"The bold fonts make the letters easy to read. And the creative illustrations make the letters easy to remember. It's a fun and easy way for anyone to learn the Arabic alphabet."

Wendy Radwan, UCLA student

"You know my husband's in the military, and when he gets deployed abroad, I want him to be able to communicate effectively and understand the culture around him.

Of course, this could also increase his safety. Definitely.

It's easy to read, and the pictures make it easier to understand and retain immediately. There's nothing else like this on the market. It is effective, and I recommend it to anyone of any age, who wishes to learn Arabic letters faster.

It's a good system!"

Lana Rapoza, housewife

"I look at it [Arabic], and the letters are like ak-ak-ak-ak, garble-garble, it's just like...upsetting. You know? Just to try to make sense out of it. ...This course will help me to achieve my goals. Excellent! Excellent!"

Robert Zuniga, executive

Go ahead and check out
http://www.authoritybooks.com/arabic.html
for some free stuff that will help you out.

AUTHORITY BOOKS, INC. AUSTIN, TX